PROMISE OF
FUTURE GLORY

PROMISE OF FUTURE GLORY
REFLECTIONS ON THE MASS

By
Cardinal Vincent Nichols

alive Publishing

First published in 1997 by
Darton, Longman and Todd Ltd
1 Spencer Court
140-142 Wandsworth High Street
London SW18 4JJ

A catalogue record for this book is available from the British
Library

Scripture quotations are taken from The Jerusalem Bible ©
1966, 1967 and 1968 by
Darton, Longman & Todd Ltd and Doubleday & Co Inc.

Front cover image: See Appendix II

Republished in 2005 by Alive Publishing Ltd,
Graphic House, Stoke on Trent, ST4 2PH
Tel:+44 (0) 1782 745600 • Fax:+44 (0) 1782 745500
Email: booksales@alivepublishing.co.uk
www.alivepublishing.co.uk

3rd Edition published in 2018 by Alive Publishing Ltd.

ISBN 978-1-906278-30-4

To my Mother and Father
My first and best teachers

CONTENTS

CONTENTS

INTRODUCTION

I am very pleased to introduce this new edition of *The Promise of Future Glory*.

I hope that the new edition can contribute to the fruitfulness of the Eucharistic Congress, Liverpool, September 2018. That Congress serves to deepen our appreciation of the central importance of the Eucharist in our life of faith, both in the celebration of the Holy Mass and in Eucharistic Adoration.

On quiet weekdays, I often celebrate morning Mass with two or three other people. In the quiet of the chapel in Archbishop's House, Westminster, we try to enter deeply into the action of Jesus, who by the great gift of himself on the Cross and by his rising to new life, gives our day its energy and meaning. The Mass is the source of our mission.

A little while ago, the refrain for the Responsorial Psalm that we said together was this: 'You are my Son; it is I who has begotten you this day' (Ps 2.6). While traditionally this Psalm has been taken to refer to King David in his defeat of his people's enemies, I pondered on these words as referring to each person who comes to Mass to find new life there. During that quiet celebration of Holy Mass, I could hear the Lord whispering to me: 'You are my son, my child. Do not be anxious. I will create you afresh this day!' This is indeed the very best foundation on which to start each day!

More often, however, I celebrate Mass in a parish, or in the Cathedral, for a particular occasion of one sort or another.

The Holy Mass then becomes a great act of thanksgiving for a particular moment in the life of a community, or a person: anniversaries, jubilees, even funerals and other moments of loss. We gather with a clear sense of God being part of the unfolding story of our lives. We thank God for that gift. Most often at these Masses, we are marking a gift of inspiration or encouragement, fashioned in the life of a person who is loved and cherished. This is a gift of holiness in our world, a gift for which we readily thank God in the celebration of the Mass.

Pope Francis has written about the gifts of holiness in his Exhortation *Gaudete et Exsultate*. He tells us how much joy he finds in contemplating holiness in the everyday lives of people: 'in those parents who raise their children with immense love, in those men and women who work hard to support their families, in the sick, in the elderly religious who never lose their smile' (para 7).

He explains to us that holiness is the action of the Holy Spirit, in the lives of saints and in the lives of so many others. Holiness, he says, 'is the message of Jesus that God wants to speak to the world by your life' (para 24).

Often our celebration of a Mass of thanksgiving is our praise of God for the holiness we see in the lives of so many people, in communities and parishes. No wonder such celebrations are full of joy!

At other times, less frequent I must admit, my celebration of Holy Mass takes place in a much larger gathering. Recently I was in Gniezno, in Poland, celebrating Mass with over 3000 people. It was remarkable! Then there have also been those remarkable World Youth Days. I can remember the feeling of wonder as I looked out over just part of the two million people gathered in Rome for the World Youth Day in the year 2000; or the gathering in Madrid which was well over one million, or again in Krakow in 2015. These are quite remarkable moments. The crowds stretch beyond the horizon, yet the sense of being together in prayer during Mass is palpable. It is hard to describe!

One image may help me to do so. It is as if an underground stream has suddenly burst through to the surface and is there, before my eyes, in all its splendour and strength. That stream has been the unseen source of water and life for so many plants and flowers enabling them to grow and bloom on an apparently barren surface. This happens only because the plants and flowers have put down deep roots. When the stream suddenly becomes visible, then the source of all that wonderful growth becomes so clear!

Faith is that underground stream. So often it lies hidden under the dryness of our daily efforts. But occasionally it bursts forth. These great celebrations of Holy Mass are such moments, when the stream of faith in Jesus breaks forth from below the surface, cascading across a vast landscape of people, refreshing them and showing the true source of so much instinctive goodness that adorns our world. How marvellous are those grand declarations of faith in Jesus! How wonderfully he restores our energy and reveals the secret source of life! It is his divine presence which fills those millions of hearts, so that they begin their long journeys home with a totally renewed spirit and joy.

These are some of the settings in which I celebrate the mystery of Christ's presence among us in the Holy Eucharist. Every celebration is, for me, an immense privilege. How wonderful that, in so many different circumstances, we can be part of this great mystery, offering ourselves to be, in the flesh of our world today, a sign and expression of the unfailing love and mercy of God for every one of us, His children! This is the wonder of the Mass that we must ponder unendingly!

For its special focus our Eucharistic Congress 2018 has held before us the rich ways in which this Eucharistic presence of Jesus continues in the Blessed Sacrament. This continuing presence of the Lord means that he is always with us in the very act of his surrender: his surrender, to the will of his Father, on the Cross; his surrender in love so that he can absorb into his very self all the sins of the world, lifting them from us and restoring us, in our repentance, to new Life; his surrender of himself into our hands, that through our taking to ourselves the real presence of his Body and Blood we may become part of him and so reborn again each day; his surrender of himself to the simple elements of bread and wine, now transformed in their substance yet remaining with all the appearances of these everyday commodities. Most wonderfully, he remains with us always, in this enduring Sacrament, through which he endears himself to us, for every day we can simply gaze on his presence, allowing him to fill our hearts and bind ourselves to him afresh.

These words of Pope St John Paul II can offer us new inspiration at this time:

'Faith demands that we approach the Eucharist fully aware that we are approaching Christ himself. It is precisely his presence which gives the other aspects of the Eucharist – as meal, as memorial of the Paschal Mystery, as eschatological anticipation – a significance which goes far beyond mere symbolism. The Eucharist is a mystery of presence, the perfect fulfillment of Jesus' promise to remain with us until the end of the world' (*Mane Nobiscum Domine*, para 16, October 2004).

To these words I wish to add words of Pope Benedict, spoken in the first homily of his pontificate, words which I dearly wish to make my own:

'I ask everyone to intensify over the next months their love and devotion to Jesus in the Eucharist and to express in a courageous and clear way their faith in the Lord's real presence.'

I pray that these few words may inspire us all to grow in our love of the most Blessed Eucharist, the font and pattern of our mission. I hope that the new edition of this book may play its small part in this great endeavour, too.

ONE
GATHERING THE PEOPLE

*...let us acknowledge our sins, and so prepare
ourselves to celebrate the sacred mysteries*

The congregation at any normal Sunday Mass is, to put it mildly, a motley crew. People come from all walks of life, all age groups, and a great variety of backgrounds. Some come in extended family groups, others have been living alone for years, some are highly content, others still searching, still others living with a profound sense of disappointment and failure. Among those to be found in the church, some live tidy and respectable lives, others are shambolic and idiosyncratic. But they gather, and together they form the Church.

Perhaps the Last Supper of the Lord was not that different. Certainly the Apostles were not a homogeneous group of like-minded people. Some were men of business, smart-witted and, we may assume, familiar with sharp practice. Others were hardened by physical labour, with little sympathy for soft talk or clever distinctions. Later, when they gathered in the Upper Room, recovering from the shock of the death of Jesus, we know that Mary, his mother, and other women were present too. These were the first gatherings of the disciples, the first congregations, of which our motley Sunday crews are the successors.

Summoned by the Word of God

The prayer of the Mass tells us how this comes about: '...you never cease to gather a people to yourself' (Eucharistic Prayer III). It is the initiative of God who calls us, through faith, to this place. We are not self-selecting. No doubt, if we were, we would find ways of making our gatherings much neater, more homogeneous. Perhaps this is why I feel a little uneasy when the group or congregation gathered for Sunday Mass consists entirely of like-minded members of a particular group, religious family or movement. Of course such groups exist and, rightly, celebrate the Eucharist together. But they are not a very representative picture of the Church, and those who habitually celebrate Mass in such a setting have an inadequate experience of the life of the Church at prayer. The Church is simply much less neat than that. It is a gathering of those drawn together not so much by shared convictions on this or that issue, but by a shared faith in Christ, present in the Word and Eucharist.

The proclamation of the Word of God summons the congregation. Formally that Word is heard in the preaching of the Church. Yet that Word is also at large in the whole of creation. It is proclaimed in a thousand different ways. Christ's invitation to 'Come and see' (John 1:39) is sometimes whispered into a sleeping ear, sometimes dropped into casual conversation, sometimes sensed in the beauty of creation, sometimes disguised in simple curiosity, sometimes the result of years of faithful loving, sometimes hidden in the routines and habits of a life-time. But all who come to Mass do so, in one way or another, as a result of that invitation, or initiative of God.

Perhaps the richness and variety of the images of God given in the Scriptures are a hint of the variety of ways in which God will get this invitation through to us. In the Scriptures God is spoken of as father, mother, husband, friend, lover. God is shepherd, farmer, housewife, potter, fisherman and metal-worker. God is also described as a scribe, book-keeper, muse, physician, judge, king and trader. And this is to recall but a few. The ways in which God touches our lives and draws us to himself are likewise rich and varied.

Often God's invitation is only barely sensed in the complexities of our daily lives. As we bustle along, our motivation is not so pure, our awareness not so keen. And so we arrive at church with a great jumble of expectations and needs.

Some come to church simply to 'get away from it all'. Time at Mass represents an island of peace in a hectic world. Here, at least, one can think one's own thoughts, stepping back from the immediate pressures of life. Others come to Mass in quite a different frame of mind. They are seeking answers. They hope that a word will be spoken which touches their anxiety, or that a notice is about to be given which will meet their needs. Such people often see the parish as a network of contacts and resources, there to bring the help without which life would be impossible. Others come looking less for help and resources and more for companionship and love. For them the parish is a friendly community in which they are known, respected and loved. It is a meeting place, in which a warm welcome is received and friendships are strengthened. Others come to Mass with only one thing in mind: to get closer to God and to know again God's presence. For them the Church is the pathway to holiness and little else matters that much. And there are others, too, who view the parish and all its activities as a kind of benign business in which they are partners or shareholders. They are on the look-out for efficiency and professionalism.

They will be the first to spot the spelling mistakes in the newsletter, or the out-of-date notice in the porch.

They are proud of their church and they want things to be just right. Then there are some who are not at all sure why they have come. Perhaps they occupy the back benches and the distant corners of the church. Their participation is, outwardly at least, far from full and enthusiastic. Yet they, too, have received the invitation from the Lord. They too have responded.

This tapestry of images, impressions and experience displays something of the diversity of the Church as it gathers for prayer. No one of them contains the whole story; none is totally right; none is wrong. Rather each one shines with some facet of the truth, with a glimpse of God's glory and of God's mercy.

But perhaps the Mass itself suggests one characteristic that we might let shape our reflections more than most.

Into the Presence of God

As we gather for the celebration of the Mass, we enter the realm of the explicitly religious. As we come into the church building, we are rightly surrounded by images and symbols speaking to us of God as the source and focus of life. That is the message of the statues, the candles, the icons and paintings. In one way or another, they all speak of the wonderful works of God. We enter the arena of explicit awareness of

God; an arena, a theatre, in which all initiative belongs to God, in which God is always the principal actor.

So the first step we take in making this entry is to re-establish a true relationship between ourselves and God. We have to enter anew, each time, into this ordering of things; God first, us second. This is achieved by the first act of the Mass itself: the simple invitation to 'call to mind our sins'.

The purpose of this invitation is to remind us of a basic truth: that we are not the ultimate source, reason or destiny of our own existence. We are not God. In being asked to acknowledge our sinfulness, we are not invited into an exercise of introspection, still less into self-doubt or guilt. Rather we are to establish again the true perspectives of our status as creatures standing before the Creator. Without this step we cannot get going: the Mass simply cannot begin.

We can reflect still further on this first step of the Mass. The exploration of the dependence of each person on God is at the heart of all religious experience. It can properly be said that the whole biblical revelation unfolds the drama of this dependence. The Book of Genesis introduces it clearly where the man and the woman hide from God rather than admit their fallibility. The closing of the Gospel of St Matthew, for example, brings the drama round full circle when the disciples fall to their knees before the risen Lord, although, comfortingly, 'some hesitated' (Matt 28:17). As we gather for the liturgy, this same drama is played out again and again. Its opening scene is always the same. The doorway through which all must enter is the acknowledgement of our dependence on the Almighty, not just in the nameless form of a higher power but named as the God of Abraham, Isaac and Jacob, the one who reveals himself definitively in the person of Jesus Christ.

Some would continue this line of thought a little further and claim that the exploration of the dependent relationship constitutes the heart of the Church's task.[1] The very physical presence of the church building is the first and important reminder of this truth. A landscape littered with church steeples and towers, as is ours, is a mark of a culture once fully aware of its dependence on God. The construction and care of a church building is, of course, a powerful act of witness to this truth. So too is the presence in a local community of people who have visibly and publicly dedicated their entire lives to the explicit service of God. For them to be readily recognisable can also serve as a public reminder of this fundamental relationship of dependence on God. Unless we acknowledge and accept the consequences of our finite nature then we remain impervious to the promises and claims of the Gospel.

1 Bruce Reed, *The Dynamics of Religion*, Darton, Longman and Todd, 1978

This testimony, in the form of buildings or persons, touches a raw nerve in contemporary Western culture. For many reasons, which cannot be explored here but are easily recognised, one of the defining characteristics of our modern way of life is a firm belief that we ought to be self-sufficient. We are convinced that intellectually we should be able to give a coherent explanation for every phenomena; emotionally we should be able to find satisfaction and maturity through our own best efforts. Even when faced with circumstances which might well lead to a recognition and exploration of dependency, such as a tragic accident or catastrophic air crash, the public response is always to demand technical explanations for the cause of the tragedy. 'Why did this happen?' is asked and answered at the level of practical cause and effect. We believe that once we have discovered the cause of the tragedy, and apportioned blame, then we will be able to ensure that it never happens again. Our self-sufficiency will be vindicated. The deeper meaning of the question is not normally faced, at least not in public debate. We do not generally reflect there on what such an event tells us about the meaning of our lives, the reality of death, the sources of hope and perseverance on which we can call. Such questions are considered irrelevant to the more important technical matters, and at best are relegated to private opinion.

This all suggests that a crucial part of the action of the liturgy is to help us explore the ways in which we are dependent on others and, more especially, on God. This must be done not so much in a clinical or psychological framework as in a spiritual manner. The task is to assist people in their search for the deeper meaning of daily experience, to see how it discloses the presence of God and to show how we find true fulfilment in greater openness to God who alone satisfies all our longing.

For the priest, and others involved in such ministry, this means dealing constantly with the realities of weakness, failure and sinfulness, as well as with the celebration of strength and gift. It requires insight and skill in these areas, a familiarity not only with the ways of God but also with the patters of human action, reaction and interaction.

A ready and necessary source of reflection in these matters is our own experience. We have strong instincts for identifying and dwelling on our own weaknesses. Some of them we know arise from the personal combination of nature and nurture which has made us who we now are. These influences seem largely beyond our refashioning: we experience ourselves as shy, or domineering; as over-sensitive or clumsy; as greedy or damagingly self-denying. We can often identify a profound insecurity which leaves us constantly in search of reassurance and encouragement. Other weaknesses and failures arise more from our history, the series of decisions we have made, the unacceptable habits formed over many years, the addictions which we have permitted, or encouraged, to take root.

Then we can widen our reflection to take in the long list of the evident weaknesses and sinfulness of the society and world order of which we are a part. So much repels: crippling poverty; the scandal amidst us; the constant horror of terrorism; the evident lack of moral standards which brings a flood of questionable material into our homes, libraries and street corners. The list is endless. Other aspects of modern living do not so much repel as simply grind people down: the constant effort of earning enough to support a family; the stress of complex relationships at home or at work; the onset of illness and old-age.

Responding in Faith

These are the kinds of issues that we bring with us into the church as we gather for Mass. We may not speak about them, but our hearts are filled, wearied or coarsened by them. We are, to some extent, listening out for a word which addresses these experiences, for such a word enables individuals to feel included in the action of the Mass, which otherwise can seem so remote. The question facing those who exercise ministry and leadership in the Church is, then, how should we respond in the life of the Church and in its liturgy to these experiences and concerns?

In the face of such a complex task, permit me to be simplistic.

It is possible to outline a limited number or patterns of response to these experiences. These different responses are not mutually exclusive and all contain elements of great worth. In fact each, when properly developed, proves to be the basis for a considerable wealth of analysis, diagnosis and suggested remedies. But the specific question we face is which of these should appropriately shape our liturgy?

In the first place, there is a range of responses which basically wants to hold on to the instinct that fundamentally human beings are good, and our condition is wholesome. As such these responses maintain that each person has within him or herself the capacity to resolve their problems. In fact, so the approach assumes, the main issue is that of finding the appropriate help, therapy, or programme which will enable the person to deal more effectively, more creatively, with a difficult situation.

This approach shapes many of our activities in the Church. Lists of action programmes, support or self-help groups can fill the church porch and newsletter. The assumption is that there is usually a solution to every problem. We are, after all, resourceful and responsible people.

A second range of responses tends to externalise the problems, or even politicise them. The fault certainly lies out there, with 'them'. 'They' might be the forces of unrestricted free-market capitalism, embodied in the multinational corporations; the influence of military dictatorships; the excessive interference of outside influences or the vested interests of a local power group. We are, after all, small cogs in a big machine. According to these approaches, as Christians it is our duty to come together and organise for change. In a democracy there are mechanisms to be operated, levers to be seized. Lobbies, petitions and demonstrations are important steps in this way of response.

The third range of responses springs from a different source. It starts with an assumption of failure and inability on our own part. Injustice, oppression and evil really are all our own fault. This pattern of responses often begins with the phrase 'If only'. The regret might be directed to each person's own behaviour or to actions in common. But unremittingly we are led to admit that the failure is ours. What is needed to solve these problems is greater effort, greater generosity on the part of all.

Forgive my excessive over-simplification. The route opened up by each of these starting points contains much that is of worth, much that can indeed lead to solutions, or the possibility of them, in many circumstances. It is important for us to be familiar with these routes, with the issues they open up and the rigour of thought each requires.

Laying Down the Heavy Load

But I would like to suggest that none of these is the approach which properly belongs to the celebration of the Mass. After all, we do not celebrate the Eucharist in order to become more in touch with our own inner experience and resources, though indeed the Mass may help us to do so. Nor is liturgy primarily the place for social analysis or education, even if both can emerge in and through the celebration of God's saving actions. Likewise, the Mass is not given so that we may sharpen our sense of personal responsibility and guilt for the ills of contemporary living.

Rather, the role of the liturgy is of another kind. Alongside all these other possibilities, its key task is to bring these matters consciously and deliberately to God and into the mystery of God's action in our lives. The shape of the Mass enables us to do just that. May I offer an illustrative image?

Many years ago I visited the cathedral in Galway. I recall well the huge mosaic of the crucified Christ which dominates the apse of the cathedral. I found it powerfully disturbing and perplexing. Why does this image so dominate our religious landscape, occupying pride of place in homes and churches? What exactly does it represent? How do we relate to that image in all its echoes and associations?

I looked round the crowded cathedral. My eye was caught by an older man, kneeling in prayer. His hands were large, cracked, hardened. To my urban eyes he seemed to be a typical farmer. He was bowed in prayer, his back stooped, perhaps from much lifting and carrying. He seemed to know the reality of burdens. He was, in fact, leaning against the back of a wheel-chair in which a younger man was sitting. It was, I assumed, his son, such were the discernable lines of familiarity and relationship between them. Perhaps it was his only son, or at least, his only remaining son, for it seemed to me that the care of this boy now fell to this man.

Catching sight of this simple and not uncommon scene, I thought I began to understand the power of the crucifix. It seemed to me that in the crucifix I could see a portrayal of this, and similar, experiences: the ways in which we can be pinned down by illness, by accident, by each other, by circumstances; the ways in which we carry each other's burdens, and offer to support each other; the ways in which we pierce each other through with shafts of neglect, harshness or frustration.

The crucifix also spoke of the setting down of these burdens, a letting go of them into the hands of the living God. The time comes when we can bear our burdens no longer. We too need to lay them down and, in return, receive consolation and strength.

This moving scene of a father and son finding a moment of rest in the image of the crucified Saviour, seemed to me to spell out so much about how we best respond to our experiences.

It is to the crucified Christ, the full revelation of the love and saving action of God, that we must come. It is there and there alone, that we can truly explore the full extent of the dependency which lies at the heart of our experience. Faith tells us that God alone is the source of faith, hope and love. The crucified Saviour makes it plain that the dynamic of God's action is to start precisely with the weak and human parts of each person, all that is sick and shall die. In this way, on this path, are the promises of life made and the revelation given. The task of the liturgy is to map out this pathway for all who take part in it. This is the beginning of the saving action of God. This is the real purpose of the invitation which has drawn us to the Church.

'Brothers and sisters, let us ackowledge our sins, and so prepare ourselves to celebrate the sacred mysteries.' This, I suggest is not simply a ritual purification. Unworthy we most certainly are. But the thrust of this opening moment is more profound that that. It asks us to face fairly and squarely the facts of our daily living. It is an invitation to lay hold of the truth of our lives and to see the true measure of our failure and of our dependence on God.

This is an important aspect of the message delivered in the Book of Revelation to the seven churches. These messages, written as warnings, prepare the churches, the people, for the coming of the Holy One. The message to the church in Laodicea reads:

You say to yourself, 'I am rich, I have made a fortune, and have everything I want', never realising that you are wretchedly and pitiably poor, and blind and naked too. I warn you, buy from me the gold that has been tested in the fire to make you really rich, and white robes to clothe you and cover your shameful nakedness, and eye ointment to put on your eyes so that you are able to see (Rev. 3:17-18).

The mystery of salvation which we are to celebrate takes precisely as its raw material our sinful and broken selves. All that we, of our human instinct, are most inclined to disown, hide or deny becomes, in God's hands, the precious stuff of our salvation. From God we receive precisely what we do not possess of ourselves. From God we receive pardon, wholeness, new integrity, peace and strength for the onward journey. As we begin the celebration of Mass we need this intense awareness of the fact that we have come here to receive. We have not gathered to celebrate our own achievements or our own sense of success. Rather we have come to be filled with that which, of ourselves, we do not have. So we gather with a readiness to listen, to be filled, to be changed.

The invitation at the beginning of the Mass asks us, then, to step up to the starting line and take our place in a Church of sinners. Then we may indeed be transformed into an instrument in the hand of God, an instrument docile to God's will and powerful with God's power alone.

Questions for Reflection

1. Are there moments when you have heard in unexpected ways the invitation of the Lord to come to church? Could you share these?

2. In the rush to get to church on time is there anything you can do, alone or with the family, to prepare for what is to come? Could you, for example, begin to shape a list of your needs and intentions for prayer?

3. What particular experience do you want to bring to Mass and lay down at the Lord's feet? Could you talk about this?

4. You may often turn to God in prayer when you feel unable to cope or painfully alone. Could you more readily turn to God in prayer when you feel full of strength or love and able to do anything?

5. In your heart of hearts, what do you expect to receive when you come to Mass?

Prayer

Lord our God, you call us into your presence, as the company of your church, to give to us your gifts of healing and grace. We stand before you with open hearts and hands. Raise our minds to you that we may hear your Word and, with all the saints, rejoice in your glory. We make this prayer through Christ our Lord. Amen.

TWO

INTO A COMMUNION
OF LIFE AND PRAYER

Let us Pray

I rather suspect that in popular opinion Christians in general, and Catholics in particular, are seen as people who, more than anything else, have additional rules to keep. This is certainly the view when it comes to sexual behaviour. Yet it is a misunderstanding. The Gospel cannot be reduced to a moral code, although a pattern of behaviour certainly flows from it.

Nor is Christianity primarily an invitation to membership of an institution with various rights and duties attached and, perhaps, some 'standing' in the eyes of others. At the heart of the Gospel lies a call which is far more important than that.

The Evangelist John puts it this way:

To all who did accept him, he gave power to become children of God (John 1:12).

It is my Father's will that whoever sees the Son and believes in him shall have eternal life (John 6:40).

If you know me you know my Father too. From this moment you know him and have seen him (John 14:7).

Eternal life is this: to know you, the only true God, and Jesus Christ whom you have sent (John 17:3).

The invitation of the Gospel, then, is not just to a particular way of life, but to radically new life itself. That life can only be described as a sharing in God's own life, an incorporation into the divine life of Father and Son and Holy Spirit. This is a life that of ourselves we can never attain. St John speaks of this invitation, this reality, in so many different ways: a vine and its branches, knowledge shared, living water quenching all thirst, bread answering all hunger, irresistible truth, new sight never to be blinded, light overcoming all darkness, love without limits, life conquering death. The call of the Gospel takes us beyond ourselves into a communion of life with God.

This, of course, is the first meaning of the much used word 'communion' or 'communio' or 'koinonia', especially when applied to the Church. The Church is a 'communion'. The Church comes about through the 'communion' of God with his people. This communion is God sharing his life with us. Now the life of God is something we perceive only dimly. We learn of it from the words and actions of Jesus. From him we know that the life of God is the life of love. We learn to speak of that love, and the truth it expresses, as flowing between the Father, the Son and the Holy Spirit. The life of God is the life of the Blessed Trinity. This is the first meaning of the Church as communion: that in the Church each person comes to share the life of God, the life of the Trinity itself.

In this perspective we begin to understand that life itself is God's first gift to us. All we are and all we have is pure gift of God. The talents which mark us out as individuals, the opportunities which come our way day by day, the context of our daily living, are all to be seen as gifts of God, given so that we might be drawn, step by step, into a fuller sharing in the life of God. For that is the very object of our existence, the purpose for which we have been created.

There is, of course, a second meaning to be found when we speak of the Church as communion. Called to share in the very life of God, we realise that we are called and gifted within the company of our fellow women and men. They too are sharers in the divine goodness. The gifts of each one are all given by God, the one source of all gifts. In a very real sense the gifts of each belong at the same time to all. We belong to each other for we all belong to one God. The gifts we have received are common property. Since all our gifts are received from the one source, then, like pieces of a jigsaw, the full picture of their purpose will emerge only when they are shared and exchanged between us. In this sense, too, the Church is a communion, a communion of gifts shared between all the disciples, who try in their lives to be a sign of the true meaning and proper use of God-given talents. In this way communion, or koinonia, is the very nature of the Church. The Church is born of the call of God. The Church is an expression of God's invitation to each person to share in the fullness of life, and, in doing so, to be drawn into wholesome relationships in the human community. The life of the Church as the sign or sacrament of all communion seeks to express and nurture this invitation by gathering together the gifts given by God, drawing them into a pattern of service, and making them, and their fruits, into a worthy offering of praise to God.

The invitation of faith, therefore, is for us to enter continually into this double communion of life: communion in the life of God and communion in the sharing of gifts in our human family. These two dimensions are, of course, inextricably bound together, just as we are taught in the great double commandment of love: love of God and love of our neighbour. Our focus is at times on God, the giver of every gift; and at times it is on each other. The invitation of the Gospel opens for us the way in which we are enabled to enter into this fullness of life: the person of Jesus himself. He alone is the revelation of the fullness of God, the opening of the path we must travel, the source of the life for which we long.

Communion and Community

The word 'communion' is very close to the word 'community'. We have toyed with this word, 'community', for years. Its meaning has been so stretched as to have been almost emptied. It is used to refer to the family, the small group, the neighbourhood, the nation state, the current European enterprise, the whole human race. We use it too, in church and parish settings. We speak, rightly, of a Eucharistic community, the people gathered together and formed by the celebration of Mass.

The sociological use of 'community' is more precise, and can help us to understand the deeper meaning of the word. I was fascinated to hear some time ago of sociological research into the experience of community within a group of parishes. As I recall, the research was based on a sociological meaning of 'community' in which some degree of personal familiarity was required. In this sense, the research found that it was extremely difficult to extend a parish 'community' beyond an invisible ceiling of three hundred people or so. Beyond that point the sense of being known and of knowing others began to dilute. The research showed that parishes working on this model of community found that despite their best efforts to recruit new members they kept coming back to this maximum figure. As new members were recruited, taking the total to well over three hundred, others left, saying that they no longer felt that special sense of belonging which they had so treasured.

The implications are clear for our particular understanding of the meaning of 'community'. If a parish is indeed to be a community, then the defining features of that community, the roots of its sense of belonging, need to be of a different order. That is not to say that personal contact, knowledge and familiarity should not be among the fruits of a parish life. But these things cannot be its aim or the source of its strength. Rather the sense of community in a parish, the experience of belonging which it offers, is to be rooted and nurtured in the double communion of life of which we have been speaking. This is what will make the parish into a true community, a Eucharistic community.

Recently I met with a group of people preparing to be received into the Catholic Church. I asked if they would be willing to share their reasons for taking this step. They were very ready indeed! One woman spoke of her experience at Sunday Mass, which she had attended with her husband and family for many years. She spoke of how she had always felt taken up and 'included' in what was going on. I asked if she was speaking about the singing, the preaching, or the sense of community'? To my surprise she rejected these alternatives and said that it was 'what went on at the altar that had always touched her deeply, and she felt taken up in that.

This woman, I believe, sensed the deeper reality of the Church. She was able to experience something of that communion of life which lies beneath many of its more outward expressions. She had a sensitivity to those realities which came through to her as an invitation, a call, to a fuller life. She was responding to that experience by seeking formally and consciously the full communion of life in the Catholic Church.

A Communion of Thanksgiving

In quite a different setting and style, St Francis of Assisi grasped these same aspirations. In his 'Prayer Inspired by the Our Father', St Frances wrote:

> May our knowledge of you
> become clearer that we may know
> the breadth of your blessing,
> the length of your promises,
> the height of your majesty,
> the depth of your judgements.

With characteristic clarity, Francis highlights exactly the source of life to which we must come. In like manner, he gave the following instruction to preachers:

> Let us refer all good to the most high and
> supreme Lord God,
> and acknowledge that every good is His,
> and thank Him for everything,
> He from Whom all good things come.
> And may He, the Highest and Supreme,
> who alone is true God,
> have and be given and receive
> every honour and reverence,
> every praise and blessing
> every thanks and glory,
> for every good is His.
> (Earlier Rule, c.1221, Chpt. xvii)[1]

Such good advice for the preacher also applies to us all. Our first duty is to give thanks to God for all the gifts that he gives: gifts that are deeply personal, gifts that come to us in and through the work of grace. We might not attain the eloquence of St Francis, but our efforts must be to express our thanks and praise as best we can, with at least a little of his infectious joy.

---

[1] This quotation and other quotations from St Francis and St Clare are taken from *Francis and Clare, The Complete Works'*, The Classics of Western Spirituality, trs. Regis Armstrong OFM and Ignatius Brady OFM, Paulist Press 1982.

A Communion of Prayer

One important way of doing this is, in fact, in prayer. Quite rightly we learn that the first purpose and dimension of all prayer is thanksgiving. When we open our mouths in prayer the first words, the first breath, the first response is to give thanks for all we are and for all we have. Other forms of prayer flow from this. But first and foremost we thank and praise God, the giver of all good things. Thanksgiving is, of course, the meaning of the word 'Eucharist'. A Eucharistic community, then, is one which gives thanks for all it has received.

The opening prayer of the Mass, the Collect, is a formal statement of the communion which is the profound reality of the Church. It is a statement, in imagery and ideas appropriate to the season, of the central mystery of our faith: the communion of life established by God's own initiative in Christ Jesus.

But I would like to draw particular attention to the first words of that act of prayer: 'Let us pray'.

In these words, the celebrant offers an invitation to the whole congregation to take the second step on the path of worship. We have gathered in faith. We have acknowledged our dependence on God. We have reached out and been grasped by God's forgiving love. Now the invitation is clear.

In this prayer we are to praise God for the gift of new life, for all the gifts of our being, our origin, our destiny. The initial invitation 'Let us pray' calls us to settle deeply into this awareness, this consciousness of God. It is a moment to put down deep roots into the living water; to feel the firmness of the bed-rock of God in our lives; to allow the light which darkness cannot comprehend to flood through our minds. It is an invitation to a moment of profound and shared communion in and before God.

The Richness of Silence

It seems to me so important that after the words 'Let us pray' there are a few moments, even a whole minute, of silence. This might seem strange, and some might begin to think that the altar missal has gone missing, or the celebrant nodded off. But the importance of these moments can easily be explained and their benefits gained.

I was deeply moved on one occasion at an early morning concelebration of Mass with the late Pope St John Paul II. At this moment in the Mass there was a pause which seemed to be almost five minutes. I became distracted, wondering what had happened. But then I gave myself to the silence. The longer it lasted the deeper it became and the more I was taken up into the prayer it contained.

In the light of this, I was fascinated to read in *Crossing the Threshold of Hope*, by Pope John Paul II, the way in which he answered the question: 'How does the Pope pray?' His answer was: 'You have to ask the Holy Spirit! The Pope prays as the Holy Spirit permits him to pray.' Perhaps these moments of silence before the Collect of the Mass were the moments in which the Pope was asking and permitting the Holy Spirit to fill his mind, his consciousness, his heart.

At the end of that celebration of Mass with the Holy Father I came away thinking that never had I been anywhere in which a sense of the suffering of the world was so keenly felt. Somehow, it seemed to me, in that small chapel there was such a concentrated awareness of all the pain, despair, and violence which is such a common part of humanity's experience. Then, much later, I came to read the rest of the Pope's answer to the question 'How does the Pope pray?' In speaking about 'what fills the interior space of his prayer', John Paul went on to explain that as Pope he was called to 'a universal prayer'. So,

the Pontiff must open his prayer, his thought, his heart to the entire world. Thus a kind of geography of the Pope's prayer is sketched out. It is a geography of communities, churches, societies, and also of the problems that trouble the world today.... All the joys and hopes as well as the griefs and anxieties that the Church shares with humanity today. (*Crossing the Threshold of Hope, p.23*)

That answer corresponded exactly to what I had experienced in those long moments of silence before the Collect.

Now obviously a private chapel, such as the Pope's, is rather different from a church full of people. Yet the invitation is the same. Each person, in his or her own way, knows something of this call to a deeper awareness of God and to the needs of daily life. These moments of silence are an important step in creating in ourselves a space, an openness, a receptivity to God. They are moments in which the particular shape of our lives can be opened before God, permitting the Holy Spirit to take hold of them. In these moments of silence we stand before the God who forgives, whose Word is about to be proclaimed, whose action we are to celebrate in the sacrament. And we do so not only as individuals, but together as the people called to this moment, this place of truth and life.

The words 'Let us pray' echo in the heart of each person present. They can set up resonances of each person's experience of personal prayer, whatever that may be. An instinct for prayer is strong in most people in church. So too is a habit of prayer even in its simplest form. This moment of the Mass is the opportunity to gather in this harvest, collecting together the prayer of everyone present. This moment is, then, an act of profound communion, a sharing of the deepest gift given by God, that of a personal relationship and communication with God. The fact that such a sharing is silent does not weaken its value. In fact, if properly understood, the silence can deepen the experience, for after these moments of shared silent prayer we are united in the one formal prayer, the Collect, which is, for that day, the common prayer of the Catholic Church throughout the world. For many people I know, this awareness of being one in prayer with the whole Church, and one with their family and friends who might be many miles away, is one of the great strengths of the practice of faith.

Prayer in Daily Life

It is also worthwhile reflecting here on the quality of prayer that is brought into those moments of silence. Prayer in daily life, for some, is a momentary pause or reflection in a hectic routine. It may or may not be accompanied by words addressed to God. But it will probably capture the essence of all prayer: raising the mind and heart to God, or at least trying to do so! For some, prayer means a morning offering, a moment in which all that the day entails is put into God's hands. For others, the best moments for prayer are when the hands are occupied but the mind is not: doing routine tasks about the house or when travelling. Sometimes the stimulus for daily prayer is the glimpse of beauty in nature, in art, or in another person. Sometimes it is the awareness of pain and suffering and of the depth of our needs. All these ways of prayer contribute to our celebration of the Mass. We bring them with us, together with all the various anxieties and worries which also move us to turn to God. To recall them, to become conscious of them, is part of our preparation for Mass, itself the supreme prayer of Christ and the Church.

Surely one of the most encouraging features of parish life in recent years is the flowering of so many ways in which people are encouraged and enabled to develop their prayer. From primary school onwards, there is much guidance and encouragement for us to come before God in a personal and open-hearted manner. Children write their own prayers. Groups experience together the initiative of the Holy Spirit in leading their prayer. The Scriptures have become a source of personal prayer in a way never experienced by many until recent years. Our own journeys of Advent and Lenten prayer, contained in the *Walk with Me* booklets and calendars have been a marvellous encouragement to many, many people. The hunger for prayer is strong in our hearts, and I know how many have benefited from this opportunity.

Other opportunities abound. The whole Ignatian tradition of prayer is so much more widely available with many centres offering guidance. *The Spiritual*

Exercises of St Ignatius Loyola can be used in a variety of situations, including in the course of everyday life, Some parishes organise 'parish retreats' and many people offer themselves as 'prayer guides'.

These and other pathways of prayer are important because they tackle the gap we experience between our faith and our daily life. Personal prayer, often springing from reflection on the Scriptures, sometimes shared with others, is a vital part of the life of discipleship. Through prayer we become more sensitive to God's presence in our lives, to our deep rooted need for God, and to the many ways in which we can respond more generously.

Young people, too, respond to such opportunities. I heard recently an experienced youth worker say that all she needed to help young people in prayer was an icon and a collection of candles. 'They are natural contemplatives' she said. The contrast with the noisy and agitated world in which we spend so much time is sharp. Perhaps it actually stimulates the need for silence and inner peace!

Parish life can respond to this need deliberately and systematically. Some parishes are establishing more opportunities for personal prayer in the parish setting. Periods of prayer before the Blessed Sacrament seem to be welcomed, with not a few parishes now undertaking long periods of such prayer. They are becoming a gathering point for many. They are truly 'schools of prayer'.

Surely one of the most important challenges for leadership in our parishes today is that of providing real opportunities for prayer. The priest, for his part, must be on the look out for ways in which this flowering of prayer can be encouraged. Clearly this is an area of church life in which a wide variety of leadership is to be found and used. Increasingly there are people trained and able to offer this leadership. These are gifts given to the Church. We should not overlook them or leave them unused.

The invitation 'Let us pray' issued by the priest each time Mass is celebrated is a call to bring the full richness of this private prayer into the action of the liturgy. The invitation is given so that the Eucharistic Prayer may be enriched by all the gifts of prayer given by the Holy Spirit. The Mass is, after all, the prayer of the whole Church. It is incumbent on the celebrant, and on those who plan the celebration with him, to be sensitive to the full implications of this invitation. Perhaps there are symbols to be used which will bring to mind other aspects of the prayer of the parish: a book of intentions, a reminder or sign of parish prayer groups. Occasionally a few words of reminder about the gathering in of all our prayer can be given, but without filling the time for silence with explanations and exhortations.

Rather, let the silence do its own work. It can speak for itself. Or perhaps the Holy Spirit can fill it. And that Spirit is surely not put off by the occasional cry of a child, or even persistent crying! My rule of thumb is that a Mass celebrated without periods of silence is robbed of a good deal of its potential. Participation does not just mean outward active participation. It can be most powerfully experienced in silence, too. And this moment of invitation to prayer is surely one of the most important occasions for such a participative silence.

These two simple phrases at the beginning of each Mass 'Let us acknowledge our sins' and 'Let us pray' closely reflect the first Gospel call, recorded by Mark:

> The time has come and the kingdom of God is close at hand. Repent and believe the Good News, (Mark 1:15).

Leadership at Mass involves enabling everyone to do precisely that: to acknowledge our true dependence before God and to open ourselves with trusting faith in prayer. In as much as these two steps are taken, we are ready to hear the Word of God. Otherwise we have simply rushed through the preliminaries.

Questions for Reflection

1. What are the best times and places of prayer for you?

2. How can you make these opportunities come about more regularly, or last a little longer?

3. What kind of help in prayer would you like to receive?

4. How could your parish Mass draw together more clearly all the prayer of the parish?

5. Which are the needs of your community, or of the world, that seem to be neglected in your own prayer and in that of the parish?

Prayer

Lord our God, to raise our minds and hearts to you is itself your gift. We thank you for this gift of prayer and praise. Give it to us in abundance that we may spend our days in joyful praise of your goodness and in seeking your help for all in need. We ask this through Christ our Lord. Amen.

THREE
HERALDS OF THE GOSPEL

Cleanse my heart and my lips, almighty God,
that I may worthily proclaim your holy Gospel

The liturgy of the Word is a most solemn part of every Mass. It is the proclamation and the breaking of the Word of God: the Word of life itself. It invites us to look closely at the central mysteries of faith, not least the invitation to 'Go, make disciples of all nations' (Matt 28:19).

In 1985, at the conclusion of a European Symposium of Bishops on Evangelisation, Pope John Paul II spoke of the need today for 'heralds of the Gospel', women and men who are 'contemplatives in love with God' and also 'experts in the human heart'.

This, of course, is the role of every Christian. By baptism we are drawn into the life of God expressed in the Word made flesh: Jesus Christ. By baptism, then, we share in that flow of love and truth which is God and which issues forth in the Incarnation. We too become participants in the mission, the sending forth, of the Son as the Light of the world. We are to play our part as 'heralds of the Gospel', making visible the presence of God in all its richness. At times this will be in a word or gesture of love or compassion; in other moments it will be by a word of truth, for truth alone can set us free. At other times we will proclaim the Gospel by reaching out through the barriers of hurt to give a touch of reconciliation or of hope. The reconciliation and hope we offer rests on the unshakable promise of life beyond every death. We will be heralds of the Gospel in endlessly different ways, in gesture, word and action, in every conceivable circumstance.

Word and Life

Two things are essential for this proclamation of the Word: a deep familiarity with that Word, and a familiarity with the condition and experience which made up daily living, spoken of by the Pope as the 'human heart'. Effective proclamation of the Word occurs when these two realities meet. It happens when the words of the Gospel seem to come true before our eyes, or when we suddenly understand a Gospel truth in the light of our own experience. At such a moment sparks fly, even as they do when two electric poles are brought into close proximity or contact. The light of the Gospel suddenly touches the reality of our life and transforms it into a conscious experience of the action of God. Then the Gospel itself comes alive with relevance and immediacy.

There is no predicting such a moment. It is a gift, a grace. It can occur, for example, in the context of personal prayer, encouraged perhaps by an imaginative use of the Scriptures. When a scriptural story is entered into and lived in the imagination, it can speak to our personal experience in a direct and remarkable fashion. Dramatic gospel stories lend themselves to this kind of prayer. The account of the attempt by the apostle Peter to walk on the water, in response to the Lord's invitation, has led many to explore in prayer the extent to which they really do have trust in God. Thomas' encounter with the risen Lord and his confession of faith has, in a like manner, helped many to come to deeper faith through imaginative prayer. The story of the woman who seeks simply to touch the hem of Jesus' garment has given heart to many who felt excluded and distanced from the Lord and unable to approach him face to face.

Such a moment of insight or realisation can also come about in conversation or even in a classroom, when a new level of understanding is achieved through a chance remark or careful study. It can even happen as the result of formal preaching, though often the insight gained is not quite the one the preacher might have had in mind!

In order to be a servant of such moments of grace, or ready to receive them, a person must seek to draw together these two poles: the dynamic of God's grace as presented in the Scriptures, and the patterns and experience of daily life. To do this a person needs to be at ease with both these sources. This does not mean being either a Scripture scholar or professor of human behavioural sciences, but it does mean having a certain 'sympathy' with both. Such sympathy, or fellow feeling, arises from an open heart and an attentiveness motivated by love. It means being prepared to approach both the Scriptures and the experience of life as holy ground, as arenas in which God is indeed at work.

Befriending the Scriptures

In approaching the Scriptures, whether during Mass or in personal reading and prayer, it is helpful to remember that they give us the definitive answer to the question: 'What happens when the love of God takes flesh in our world?' The Scriptures answer that question in the history of the Chosen People, and above all, in the words and action of Jesus himself. The Scriptures also unfold the meaning and implications of that answer, announcing its radical consequences, inviting all to share in its truth. They lay bare the dynamic of the 'work of God', the patterns which occur in the lives of all who are caught up in it. Over and over again we see that the sick are healed, the broken-hearted are restored, the arrogant are challenged, the comfortable are disturbed, the repentant sinners are forgiven and promises are fulfilled.

When our daily experience is brought into the light of the Scriptures we begin to see how similar patterns are present there too. Perhaps their dynamic is more difficult to perceive, their outcome more ambiguous than the scriptural fullness of revelation. But God's Spirit is indeed at work in our daily lives, writing a living gospel there too. We come to recognise this daily gospel, written only in small print, by the light of the definitive revelation of Christ, which is written in bold capitals. The dynamic of God's work is to be found in our daily experience, in its moments of healing and restoration, of crisis or challenge, and of fidelity and love.

Every aspect of our struggle for authentic human growth can be 'read' in this light of the Gospel. The power of the Spirit is to be found, for example, in the ways in which our struggle with evil is traced out. Legacies of damage and hurt have to be surfaced and acknowledged before they can be healed. This may take place within the trust and security of a marriage relationship, or it may be found in the confidentiality and professional skill of a period of counselling. In other circumstances such a process may be attempted at a more public level. Recently, for example, in South Africa a Truth and Reconciliation Commission was established. Its purpose was to hear, record and investigate incidents of violence, cruelty, torture and exploitation which took place during the years of apartheid. Accounts of its work are both moving and revealing. It is not difficult to read in them a testimony to the work of the Holy Spirit as people struggle to face the horrors of their recent past and move gradually towards acknowledgment and reconciliation.

In like manner, our struggle to overcome temptations to all the false promises of security, power and influence are part of the text of this living gospel. And the ultimate enemy, death, has to be looked in the face before the script of the living gospel of our lives is complete.

Yet to sense how this work of salvation is being unfolded even now in our lives is to share in the living proclamation of the Gospel. Such is the call of each of the baptised.

In today's Church there is a welcome increase in desire to know and use the Scriptures. This is surely one of the great fruits of the renewal called for by the Second Vatican Council. At every level, the Scriptures have taken a more prominent place in study, personal prayer and liturgy. Such a familiarity with the Word of God is, of course, a basic necessity for those who are to be heralds of the Gospel. It is not just a question of knowing the key content of the Scriptures, or of being able to answer enquirers' questions. It is much more a matter of being caught up in the Scriptures, of being able to recognise the scriptural themes, even when they are present in other words and circumstances. It means feeling at home with the Scriptures, especially with the Gospels, so that in our minds and hearts there is a working relationship between those stories and events of daily life.

Such a familiarity does not come easily. Attentive listening to the Word of God is essential. Hence the importance of the careful reading of that Word at every celebration of Mass. Careful reading and careful listening, both an exercise of love, can indeed prepare us to sense and heed the action of God in our lives.

Attentiveness to the Word in personal prayer is particularly essential for all who wish to be its heralds. Traditionally, the first moments of the day have been given to this purpose. Perhaps this is not possible for everyone; circumstances may not permit it to be so. But time must be found for quiet reading of the Scriptures and reflection on them. The great preacher of the Word, Dietrich Bonhoeffer, reminds us of the priority of this task and of why, if at all possible, it should have first place in the day. He insisted that the first moments of the day were not a time for his own plans and worries, not even for his own zeal; but for God's Word. Before we approach the day, we should approach the Lord.[1]

Befriending Our Experience

Growing in familiarity with the Word of God is but one of the two poles we are considering. The other is the reality of daily life. How do we approach this? How do we bring the two together? Here, perhaps, lies the key to effective proclamation of the Gospel.

Many words have been written on this gap between Gospel and life. For some it is the critical issue of our time, as increasingly public perceptions of reality, and comment upon events, include no acknowledgment of the realities of faith. The world of daily phenomena is seen to be whole and entire in itself, requiring no explanation or reflection other than the pragmatic and scientific. The undoubted autonomy of secular disciplines has grown into their claim to be the sum total of all the knowledge and truth accessible to human beings.

There are, perhaps, a number of ways in which this gap can be addressed. We can approach it in terms of the events of daily life, for it is possible to reflect on those events in such a manner as to see how they do

---

[1] D Bonhoeffer, *Meditating on the Word*, Cowley Publications 1966

indeed relate to the events and truths of the Gospel. This has often been done in radio programmes such as 'Thought for the Day', or 'Pause for Thought' or the late-night 'Epilogue' that used to mark the end of television programmes for the day. These moments require a re-reading of the news, not for its sensationalism, nor for its scientific or financial implications. Rather it has to be re-read to see where the events of the day point to, or bear, some of the truths of the Gospel. It is these truths, hidden in the text of daily events, which need to be brought to the surface, so that the work of God may be recognised and a prayer of thanksgiving offered.

The same task of reflecting on daily events in the light of the Gospel is undertaken in many parishes and Christian organisations. Sometimes this can happen in a parish when a group meets week by week to prepare the Sunday Mass readings. As part of that preparation the members of the group can also share their reflections on how the scriptural texts relate to the events of the week, as talked about in the launderette or at the street corner. Many helpful themes for Sunday homilies have emerged from such discussions!

Befriending Our Culture

Yet there is another level at which the Gospel must be brought into contact with daily living. Beneath the events which make up the news of the day, at the level of both national news and neighbourhood gossip, there is a matrix or network of assumptions and values underpinning all the stories. News is spread precisely because it cuts against, or strongly confirms, the assumptions and expectations of our way of life. Such underlying patterns of life are sometimes spoken of as our 'culture', the somewhat hidden and unexamined ways in which we do things. The greatest challenge of evangelisation is to bring the Gospel to bear on these hidden assumptions. Pope Paul VI reflected on this problem in his great document on evangelisation, *Evangelii Nuntiandi*. He wrote:

> What matters is to evangelise culture and cultures (not in a purely decorative way as it were by applying a thin veneer, but in a vital way, in depth and right to their very roots), in a wide and rich sense, always taking the person as one's starting-point and always coming back to the relationships of people among themselves and with God.

> The split between the Gospel and culture is without a doubt the drama of our time, just as it was of other times. Therefore, every effort must be made to ensure a full evangelisation of culture, or more correctly, of cultures. They have to be regenerated by an encounter with the Gospel (*Evangelii Nuntiandi, para. 20*).

Part of our problem in tackling this challenge is, of course, that we are so caught up in our daily living that we find it difficult to step back and see its shape and patterns. We are so much a part of the culture in which we live that we cannot easily identify it. That culture informs and shapes all our assumptions and starting points. It gives a selected emphasis to certain values or principles; it downplays others. We are hardly aware of it, so much has it become simply our way of doing things.

Some time ago, however, I heard a presentation which helped me greatly to become aware of the culture of which I am part.[2] Interestingly, this approach had been developed in the context of missionary work in unfamiliar cultures. In order to understand the lives of the people to whom they had gone, missionaries developed these simple steps. These same steps are useful for us in coming to see and understand our own culture. They can help us to 'step outside' our way of life for a moment and approach it with fresh eyes. Then we can begin to see some of its underlying patterns. Then we can bring it to meet the Gospel.

This approach uses seven verbs as seven windows through which to see more clearly into a culture. Each verb describes an aspect of life and is used as a pathway along which to approach that culture. Each

---

[2] This presentation was given by Paul Heibert at a conference entitled 'Faith and Culture' in October 1990

can be envisaged as one side of a many-sided sphere, or as a window which enables us to look into that way of life. Together they reveal the whole, yet each highlights an important aspect of life as lived in this particular culture.

In the rest of this chapter I will take each of these verbs and indicate briefly how, by bringing it to the Gospel, a new and redeeming light can be cast on our daily living. Each verb opens up an important aspect of our lives. The Gospel challenge to it is direct and radical. Only gradually will the Gospel permeate and change us.

Identity

The first of these key verbs is 'to be'. The questions it raises are those of kinship, identity, belonging. In our way of life, how is a person's identity constructed? What are the key elements of that identity? How would a person go about answering the question, 'Tell me, who are you, where are you from?'

It is perfectly clear that different cultures answer this in different ways. I remember well the Kenyan athletics team at the 1992 Olympic Games. One of the athletes was involved in a controversial incident which probably cost him a medal. But all requests for interviews with the athlete concerned were refused. He saw himself simply as a member of a team. If any action was to be taken, it would involve the whole team, and not him as an individual.

In sharp contrast to this, identity in Western European cultures is very much focused on the individual. No doubt family and social ties will be acknowledged and explored as giving greater richness and depth to an individual. For some, great emphasis will be placed on the school which a person attended as an important factor accounting for his or her sense of self. For others, a key feature might be the football club, town or village to which a person gives his or her allegiance. But at the heart of identity lies the individual, alone and complete.

On the basis of this sense of identity, other aspects of life begin to emerge. For example, identity and loyalty often go hand in hand. These are powerful sources of deep feelings and commitments. Heroic self-sacrifice, for example, for the sake of one's loved ones is a feature of many a family or nation's history. So too the question of identity often lies at the heart of conflict and violence. The rise of divisive nationalism, or the conflicts which have so marked life in Northern Ireland, can be seen as rooted in questions of identity, stretching back over many generations.

In asking the questions which arise from the verb 'to be' not only do we begin to appreciate a way of life, but we also begin to get in touch with some of its energy and passion.

Yet, when we look to the Gospel for an understanding of identity and belonging, a very different picture emerges. The contrast is sharp, for the Gospel offers a radical alternative identity, dependent not on personal history or status, but on the action of God. My own sense of identity, then, shaped so profoundly by the culture of which I am a part, contrasts to that sense of identity which arises from the Gospel. When Nicodemus first hears of this new identity he cries out, 'But how can anyone who is already old be born? Is it possible to go back into the womb again and be born?' (John 3:4-5) Yet the Gospel proclaims that we are indeed a new people, and that a new kinship exists between us all. That kinship is announced at the foot of the cross when Jesus invites John to see in Mary his mother, and Mary to see in John her son. The first community of disciples, assembled there at the foot of the cross, at the birth of the Church, have to learn that the bonds which bind them together in Christ are stronger than those of blood and upbringing. For these bonds of new life come from God and will endure into eternity.

Activity and Esteem

The second verb which can be used as a window or a way into a culture is the verb 'to do'.

Many people feel some discomfort when asked, rather directly, 'Well tell me, what do you do?', for the question raises the issue of what a particular society, or culture, regards as being a worthy occupation. I can recall some households I have known as a priest in which books were not permitted. Reading was not a worthy occupation. In others, of course, any manual work is looked upon with some scorn.

It is not hard to detect in contemporary Britain the high esteem in which wealth creation is held. In consequence, those who play no obvious part in that process, or whose contribution is at best indirect, are often left feeling unappreciated. Mothers, or fathers, dedicating their time to the upbringing of their children, forsaking promotion or prosperity, are not given a ready hearing. Nor too are many in the 'softer' professions, such as teachers, social workers or nurses. A society which is increasingly geared towards immediate wealth creation and the satisfaction of market demands will value the related occupations much more than others.

Yet the Gospel revelation gives us quite a different outlook on the meaning of our activity and productivity. We are stewards of this created world. We have responsibilities towards it which we fail to honour if our aim is simply to use the created world for our own advantage. Again and again the gospels tell us not to attribute too much importance to our search for security or wealth. 'What does it profit you?' we are asked with an insistence that is telling. This is almost the first lesson that the apostle Peter has to learn. After slaving fruitlessly all night for his regular catch of fish, Jesus provides it for him in a moment. In doing this Jesus puts before Peter new perspectives on the nature of worthwhile activity, changing all his previous assumptions and bringing him to a new way of life. For us, too, such a change of perspective can be liberating and redemptive.

Truth and Knowledge

Moving round the surface of the sphere, we come next to the third of these 'entry verbs'. It is the verb 'to know'.

Reflect for a moment on the way in which, in your experience, you come to knowledge, and the basis on which you give credence. For many readers the process will be one centred round the evidence of your own senses and thoughts. Does this make sense to you? Does it correspond to your experience? Does it feel right?

A shift in emphasis takes place when the question is posed in the public arena. The expert who is invited onto the television programmes is invariably the person who has observable or researched evidence to present. Authority is given to the facts. The source of truth is research and experimentation. 'Public truth', for the most part, is limited to information. The interpretation of that information is a matter of debate and, in the end, of personal opinion. Take, as an example, the questions about the beginnings of human life. Those who have observable evidence to present are listened to. Yet the meaning of those awesome pictures taken within the womb, and the value to be given to the life that is to be seen there is regarded as a matter of personal opinion. In our culture, then, truth, in the public forum, is narrowly defined. Private opinion, and behaviour based upon it, is given free range.

The challenge of the Gospel is no less radical when it comes to these questions. Quite simply, all authority is claimed for Christ as the focal point of God's saving action. In Christ not only is the truth of God revealed, but the truth about the human person also is declared. Perhaps this challenge hits home most of all in its insistence that we come to knowledge of the truth about ourselves and our world not by our own efforts, but by a revelation, a giving of the truth. This does not excuse or remove from us the responsibility of trying to uncover and understand that truth. Indeed every effort we make to reflect on and understand our life experience, all scientific endeavour and artistic achievement, every effort to find coherence and meaning, are places of God's self-disclosure. But the Gospel requires of us a fundamental attitude of acceptance and reverence before the truth as given. Gospel, or revealed truth, then, has an objective quality. It is more than my discovery. How we gain access to that source of truth, the ways in which it is mediated to us, and the points at which we are able to test our understanding with a degree of certainty, all require careful thought and firm belief. They are issues central to our understanding of the Church and the authority given to the Church by Christ.

The fundamental Gospel perspective, then, is that truth is offered as an invitation. Taking up that invitation will mean being a servant of the truth and never its owner or master. This contrasts sharply with the expectations and demands of contemporary cultures which continually propose human endeavour as self-sufficient and, indeed, self-fulfilling. In the light of the Gospel, truth is not simply a discovery, but fundamentally it is a gift. And it is given in Christ.

Relationships

The next verb which serves as a window into our way of life is the verb 'to relate'.

Anthropologists and social scientists have long been fascinated by the variety of ways in which a society is ordered. Not only can external patterns of relations be observed, but the values underlying those patterns can be identified. For example, at present it is not difficult to see participants in the market. Poverty, then, excludes not only from market activity, but sooner or later from public and political life too. Not surprisingly, the proclamation of the Gospel bears directly on our understanding of these relationships. There are many biblical images to remind us that the ways in which we belong to one another and relate to one another are much deeper than market forces and economic participation. The Scriptures provide us with many positive images of our common household, such as Christ as the cornerstone of our communal life (Eph 2:20); and they give us negative images too, such as the Tower of Babel (Gen 11). These can serve as warnings: when the sense of common life and common good is lost, and fundamental perspectives are mistaken or neglected, then disruption of public relationships will most surely follow.

Enjoyment and Play

A fifth verb which opens for us an important dimension of a culture is the verb 'to play'. Leisure is an important part of every way of life, even if in our pressurised society it is somewhat neglected by many. Even so, the way in which leisure and play is understood reveals a great deal about a particular culture. One has only to think of the book or the film *A Clockwork Orange* to realise that in some settings 'leisure', or 'play', can become inherently destructive.

In contrast, a constructive instinct should lie at the heart of pleasure and play for they require both imagination and creativity. Yet increasingly there seems to be an expectation that leisure is a product to be provided and consumed, rather than creative activity. Children, perhaps, are the best teachers here. At play they often require only the simplest of props, and, at their best, they can delight in and share hours of joyful entertainment.

In this, children are also teachers of the Gospel, for one of the most neglected of all the Gospel perspectives is that concerning our attitude to relaxation and play. Only a firm sense of God as Lord of all can free us for relaxation. Otherwise we have a crushing sense that everything is dependent on ourselves. What a contrast to the attitude of the saints! They seemed to be able to live with a freedom born of profound trust.

The Book of Genesis reminds us that Adam and Eve lost their delight in the Garden of Eden precisely when they reached out for an illusory self-sufficiency. Then, it would seem, their capacity for unfettered joy disappeared. Similarly, the Book of Wisdom makes clear that one of the truths at the heart of all reality is that God is at play in all creation (Wis 6-9). So much around us can be a source of uncomplicated joy: the beauty of nature, the thrill of competition, the delight to be found in friendship, the pleasure of music and the creative arts. If we are to enter the mystery of life more fully we need to be doing serious things more lightly and light things more seriously: at least, such is the invitation of the Gospel. It has been suggested that the one question we will be asked by God at the moment of our judgement is: 'Did you enjoy my creation?'

Suffering and Death

The next window through which we must take a brief glimpse is the verb 'to suffer'. How do we handle suffering and pain? How do we respond to each other's experience of illness? Are public reactions to suffering and death different to private responses?

This, of course, is an immense and rich theme which discloses a great deal about a way of life.

For many today the natural instinct to avoid pain and discomfort has become an absolute. Pain is simply meaningless and it is to be avoided at all costs. This is the central appeal of the euthanasia lobby, which argues that the avoidance of pointless pain permits the deliberate and direct ending of life. Death, too, is held to be distasteful and best kept out of sight if at all possible. How revealing it is to hear nurses say that some people refuse to come and visit their very elderly relatives as they approach death, saying, 'we would rather remember them as they were'.

Increasingly I meet people who have never been with a person as they died and have never seen a dead body. Our society seems to be intent on shutting away all signs of suffering, decay and death.

I heard not so long ago that in Sweden funeral rites were becoming less common. Rather than remembering those who had died, some wish now simply to forget them. The task of the undertaker is no longer that of preparing for a ceremonial ending and remembering, but that of removing all signs, all memories of the deceased. Apparently such is the custom among some African tribes, when on the death of a person all their possessions are burned along with the body. The ritual simply says, 'It is over. There is no more.'

Indeed, who will ever forget the witness given by Pope John Paul II in the final weeks and days of his life? His determination not to hide his suffering and physical decline was remarkable. Indeed some would say that the silent witness of his final appearances and blessings touched the nerve of our society more deeply than many of his other actions. The Christian approach to suffering and death is in sharp contrast to these emerging patterns.

In this way, some of life's harsher experiences are to be approached in the light of the Gospel images of pruning the vine that it might produce more fruit. In life and in faith, we are often brought to the foot of the cross, to reflect again and again on the fact that the pathway to the fullness of life goes over the hill of Calvary. There is no avoiding it. Yet the Good News announced by the Gospel is that Christ has already travelled that road, embracing its horrors. In our journey, then, we are not alone; and we have caught a glimpse of its eventual outcome. This changes profoundly our attitudes to suffering and death. No longer are they meaningless. Rather, they are stepping stones to future glory. This Gospel of life challenges very directly so many contemporary trends. It is lived heroically by all who sustain their care for the sick and the elderly, whether at home or in institutions, and by those who accompany others at the hour of their death.

Worship

Finally, and not surprisingly, there is the verb 'to worship'.

In every experience of life there seems to come the point at which knowledge and skills fail and we are left with a keen sense of our inadequacy. How do we respond to that? Likewise there are inevitably moments when we sense that the sum total of our experienced world is insufficient for the longing, or space, that seems to exist within us. There is, indeed, an instinct for the transcendent lurking within each of us. We recognise the feeling that there is more to life than this present moment, and that we can indeed reach beyond it to a greater reality, a greater truth. Many have written about such 'intimations of immortality' and many have observed the great variety of ways in which societies have responded to that instinct and need.

The Gospel message addresses this directly. In his gospel, St John returns again and again to a key phrase. It occurs, for example, at the time of Our Lord's prayer in the garden just before his arrest. Judas approaches bringing with him the Temple guard. Jesus says:

> 'Who are you looking for?' They answered, 'Jesus the Nazarene'. He said 'I am he'. Now Judas the traitor was standing among them. When Jesus said, 'I am he', they moved back and fell to the ground (John 18:5-6).

A closer reading of this text reveals that the key phrase is 'I am he'. It is a direct echo or repetition of the divine name revealed to Moses when he boldly asks God to tell him who he is (Exod 3:13-14). On hearing this phrase 'I am he', and realising its implications, Judas and his company fall to the ground. The gospel is proclaiming that Jesus is the Lord, the one who alone is to be worshipped, for in him is found the fullness of the Godhead. He then is the one who satisfies our deepest longings. He is the focal point of all true worship, freeing us from all false idols.

The paradox of Christian worship, which makes it so difficult for the modern mind, is that this Jesus is soon to be seen as a broken man, scourged, mocked, humiliated and crucified. The invitation to worship him alone turns on its head our instinct about power and prestige.

This Gospel truth is hard to accept in a society which is as preoccupied as ours is with power and status. True worship serves no other purpose than giving glory to God. True worship not only responds to that deeply seated instinct in each of us, it also refines and reshapes that instinct, revealing the name of the one who is alone to be worshipped and the new order of life which is God's gift. Attentiveness to this priority will constantly purify our worship, removing from it our desire to impress and put on 'a good show'.

Proclaim the Good News

This brief and inadequate sketch might help to highlight some of the points of creative contact between our way of life and the Gospel. These points are to be found in the lives of each of us, day by day. Our conversations are made up of these matters, clustering round these different verbs, in one guise or another. Bringing a Gospel perspective to each of them helps to make clear the wonderful invitation of the Gospel to newness of life. But I hope it also demonstrates, on reflection, the fact that in every culture, in every way of life, traces of Gospel truth are already to be found. Great generosity, self-sacrifice, courage in the face of suffering, infectious joy in life, are to be found in so many situations. These qualities are rightly spoken of as 'seeds of the Word', reflecting in a small way the full glory of the Word revealed in Christ. Part of the task of the 'preacher', whether that task is fulfilled in a pulpit or, more likely, in an office canteen or supermarket, is always to acknowledge this gracious presence of God as a starting point for its fuller proclamation.

Hearing the Word of God, reflecting on it with heart and mind, listening to the homily, are important moments in the celebration of Mass. Indeed they are preceded by the recitation by the priest, or deacon, of a rather lovely prayer. It reads:

> Cleanse my heart and my lips almighty God,
> that I may worthily proclaim your Gospel.

This is a prayer which can be used whenever we approach the Scriptures, for study, for private prayer or contemplation, as well as during Mass. It is a prayer which is relevant to every Christian, called to proclaim these Gospel truths. Our listening to them, with heart and mind, is crucial preparation and nourishment for that task.

This prayer is easily learned by heart. To say it often will not only help us to receive the Word, but also to be its heralds, day by day.

Questions for Reflection

1. Which parts of the Scriptures do you find most helpful as a starting point for prayer? Is it the words of St Paul that you can think about? Is it the Gospel stories that you can enter into in your imagination?

2. Have you ever experienced a moment or event that seemed just like a Gospel story come alive?

3. Can you think of another person who seems to embody something of the light or compassion of Christ? Could you share your thoughts with others?

4. Can you think of moments when it was probably right to speak 'words of faith' to another person yet you failed to do so?

5. Do you understand a little better now the culture of which you are a part? If so, in what ways?

6. In what ways to you think your culture and the Gospel are pulling in opposite directions?

7. Is there some activity for your parish to undertake that would bring the Gospel into closer context with the culture of these times? Does one of the seven verbs used in this chapter help to suggest any such activity?

Prayer

Lord our God, you call us to be heralds of your good news in our world today. Give us minds that are open to your Word and to the realities of your world. Give us eyes to discern your presence in every place. Give us hearts warmed by your love and ready to respond in generous service to all who are in need. We make this prayer through Christ our Lord. Amen.

FOUR
NAMING THE NAMES

I believe in one God, the Father Almighty...
in one Lord Jesus Christ, the only Begotten
Son... I believe in the Holy Spirit

E ach of the authors of the first three gospels, Matthew, Mark and Luke, bring together the various sayings of Jesus into collections. These collections give us vivid pictures of the people gathered round the Lord, listening to his teaching. The best known example of this is, of course, the Sermon on the Mount (Matt 5-7).

Interestingly, after each of these early presentations of the teaching of Jesus, the gospel writer informs us that Jesus wanted to move on. Jesus tells his disciples that they are going to cross the Sea of Galilee, to 'go to the other side' (Mark 4:35; Matt 8:18). It is as if the preaching of the Gospel contains within itself the imperative to move on, to reach out ceaselessly to more and more people.

In the gospel of Luke, the element of journey plays an even more central role. It gives shape to the whole gospel, and the collections of the teachings of the Lord are given in the context of this journey:

> Now after this he made his way through towns and villages preaching, and proclaiming the Good News of the kingdom of God (Luke 8:1).

Yet in this gospel too, after the preaching of the Lord has been presented, the special journey across the Sea of Galilee is to be made.

The Sea of Galilee is really quite small. But it is large in significance. The believer must be ready to leave the homely and the familiar, such as was the village of Capernaum, and be prepared to strike out into the unfamiliar and the hostile. For the lake, though small, had a reputation for unexpected and violent storms. And this is precisely what happens to the disciples. In no time at all a heavy storm hits the disciples' boat and they begin to ship water (Luke 8:22). The disciples begin to panic, which, considering some of them were fishermen by trade, is an indication of the severity of their predicament. They are not helped by the fact that Jesus is sound asleep in the stern of the boat.

The calming of this storm at the command of Jesus is, of course, an invitation to us all to put our trust in him. We need constantly to hear his authoritative command: 'Be calm'.

Yet facing and overcoming the storms of life is not the only truth being unfolded for us in this gospel story. The disciples' journey is not yet complete. Their destination is 'the other side'. And the other side of the lake was unknown and hostile territory. That is where they must go. The Gospel message has to be taken even there.

The minute they stepped ashore their worst fears must have been fulfilled. For there, confronting them was the most fearsome of characters, the Gerasene demoniac. The gospel accounts are vivid:

> No sooner had he left the boat than a man with an unclean spirit came out from the tombs towards him. The man lived in the tombs and no one could secure him any more, even with a chain; because he had often been secured with fetters and chains but had snapped the chains and broken the fetters, and no one had the strength to control him. All night and all day, among the tombs and in the mountains, he would howl and gash himself with stones (Mark 5:2-5).

This, then, is the point of their journey. They have been brought face to face with the forces of destruction and with all that is most alien. The Gospel must be brought here, to this desolate place, to confront the diabolic. If the disciples had found the storm distressing, this was simply terrifying.

Facing up to Evil

The routines of daily living followed by most people give reasonable shelter from exposure to such extremes of disintegration and distress. But they are not unknown. At one time or another, many come face to face with such realities. Millions of people in the last century alone have experienced unambiguous evil in the events of war. For others, evil has entered their lives when they have been subjected to criminal assault and violence. To a lesser degree, a short walk taken by many along the streets of most major cities, especially at quiet times of the day or night, will involve meeting, or avoiding, people whose way of life might seem to be odd. There may even be more than a hint of threat in the air. In families, lives disintegrate under personal, economic and social pressures. The breakdown of a marriage, for example, can gradually destroy not only a couple's relationship but also their inner stability, the self-confidence of their children and their social standing. When that happens all the power and creativity of love can turn into a force for destruction and revenge, even if the controls of society limit its outward expression. Our world is indeed marked by the forces of disintegration.

So often our first reaction is to attempt to contain and control these forces of disintegration. We attempt to put things to rights. Sometimes it works. More often it does not. I recall vividly, as a young priest, rushing to the help of a parish sister who was being verbally abused at the door by a man of the road rather the worse for drink. Telling him off roundly for speaking in that way to a nun, I eased him off the doorstep – or pushed might be more accurate – and quickly shut the door. 'There was no need for that' said Sister Mary, 'it doesn't help'. Sure enough, six seconds later, the panels on either side of the front door were kicked in, glass showering everywhere.

Such lessons teach us, little by little, greater familiarity with these destructive powers. Then we gradually come to recognise them in less dramatic and more familiar circumstances. The factions which build up in family, school staff-room or parish are often fuelled by some fairly basic and raw emotions: jealousy, anger, resentment. While the restraints of virtue and social expectations normally keep such forces well in check, it is not difficult to glimpse their power. We can also come to see the same dynamics at work within ourselves, within our own hearts, for we too are subject to these same forces and temptations.

It is times and experiences such as these which illustrate well the literal meaning of the word 'diabolic'. It means 'to throw apart'. That is precisely what happens. When I am in the grip of such emotions and reactions, then I do indeed sense a tearing apart of the world as I know it. The fury of a child in a tantrum probably knows no bounds. It can be frightening enough for an adult. It must be terrifying for a child, which explains, perhaps, why the child will come for reassurance and love once the furies are spent.

Naming the Names

After the vivid portrayal of demoniacal fury, echoes of which we can indeed recognise in our own circumstances, the gospel story is also important for what happens next.

> Catching sight of Jesus from a distance, he ran up and fell at his feet and shouted at the top of his voice, 'What do you want with me, Jesus, son of the Most High God? Swear by God you will not torture me!' For Jesus had been saying to him 'Come out of the man, unclean spirit'. 'What is your name?' Jesus asked. 'My name is legion' he answered 'for there are many of us' (Mark 5:7-9).

We are now approaching the heart of this encounter with the forces of evil: the naming of the names. The spirit of evil is able to recognise and declare the true name of Jesus, something which is as yet beyond his disciples. Jesus, in his turn, evokes the name of those destructive forces. The stage is now set for the heart of the confrontation. We know exactly where we are.

The naming of names is very much part of the function and role of religious faith. Through faith we are given the gift of being able to name God. Through faith we recognise God as the author of all goodness, beauty and truth. Through faith we acknowledge the name of Jesus, at which every knee shall bend (Phil 2:10-11), and we may even bow our heads. At baptism we receive a name, strengthened or embellished at confirmation. And we read in the Book of Revelation that when we come into the full presence of our Lord and God, then the name held for us in all eternity will be revealed (Rev 2:17). In the declaration of each name, something of the truth is being expressed and grasped. In naming the names we are being brought into a deeper understanding of what otherwise might well remain a confusion or at least a puzzle. Our understanding of a person begins to take shape around the name that person bears. The beauty of creation is clarified when we see it as the handiwork of God. The naming of sin, too, helps us to be clear about the choices we have made or, indeed, the feelings we may be experiencing.

Making Sense of Life

One image by which we can visualise this aspect of religious faith is that evoked by a slide projector. If the projector lens is not quite in focus, then the slide will be fuzzy and indistinct. The picture will be there, but it will be difficult to interpret or enjoy. The function of religious faith is somewhat like the step by which the lens of the projector is adjusted and the slide brought into sharp focus. Then the picture can be seen for what it is. Its true features are clear. It can be properly appreciated.

In this sense the task of faith is to bring coherence and light to our experience. It enables us to see the connections in our experience, the patterns of good and evil that interweave in daily life. It brings the light of revelation to our task of making sense of what happens to us, our joys, sorrows, hopes and anxieties. By faith we can name and appreciate the goodness of God, coming to us through the hands and hearts of those around us. We are also enabled to name the sinfulness, the evil which we confront, both in our own hearts and in the patterns of community and public life. Faith, too, helps us to find our way through the many ambiguities which characterise our daily experience, without ever completely reducing them to simple alternatives, for that clarity comes only in the light of the full presence of God. But at least we know where to go with these ambiguities, bringing them as fully as possible through prayer, discussion and discernment into the light of faith and the judgement of the Gospel.

In these ways it is right to speak of faith as 'symbolic'. Faith is the opposite of the diabolic, for faith serves to draw together and reveal the inner harmony and unity of life. In revealing the name of God, as creator of all things, it reveals the inner coherence of the created order. In speaking of Christ, the Eternal Word, it exposes the hidden purpose and destiny of that creation. Such is the meaning of the word 'symbolic': to draw together, to bring into coherence.

The Creed

The liturgical moment which corresponds to this aspect of faith is the proclamation of the Creed. In the Creed we declare our faith in the initiative of God, and unfold the God-given plan and purpose of our lives. In this sense the articles of the Creed are 'symbolic'. They are the gathering points of faith and meaning. Not surprisingly, the Latin title of a creed is *symbolum fidei* – the symbol of faith.

Understood in this way, it is not at all surprising that the proclamation of the Creed comes immediately after the proclamation of the Word. In the dialogue of Word and daily life we have been trying to bring together this particular passage of Scripture and our particular experience of life. We have sought the creative interaction of God's Word for our lives which reveals God's presence in our daily living. In this way we consciously bring to our lives the demands of the Gospel. Now, in the proclamation of the whole Creed, we step back from such particulars and sketch out again the whole sweep of faith, celebrating the coherence of life which arises from it.

The Creed is our attempt to get our act together. It is a proclamation of identity, a celebration of who we are. I recall well a moment in a recent ecumenical conference. Each of the participants was asked to give a succinct statement of their faith. Some presented formal documents in which the particular Church, or denomination, expressed its self-understanding. Some of these documents were to be signed by those who joined that denomination. I tried to explain that the only equivalent statement I could refer to was the Nicene Creed or the Apostles' Creed. But neither of them I insisted were to be signed. Rather they were to be sung. The 'symbol of faith' is not so much a statement as a proclamation. It is, indeed, a hymn of praise.

The pulling power of the Creed is quite remarkable. It literally pulls together people who, at a different level, differ from each other quite remarkably. The proclamation of the Creed is a revelation, and a celebration, of all that unites Christian disciples, even when other disagreements or conflicts might be pushing them apart. As a young seminarian, I remember attending some of the celebrations of Mass during the Second Vatican Council. I recall my sense of wonder at seeing various cardinals, such as Cardinal Ottaviani and Cardinal Suenens, celebrating Mass together, reciting the same Creed, when all the Catholic world was learning about how deeply they disagreed over so many issues. I can recall, too, much more recently, on the eve of the visit of Pope John Paul II to Britain, how Mass was celebrated at St Peter's by Cardinals from Britain and Argentina: two countries which had just declared war. Their joint proclamation of the one Creed illustrated well its symbolic power. War was driving two countries apart. But at another level, these representatives of the two countries could declare their profound unity of faith and vision. Ambiguities are not removed, but the symbol is powerful to act if we let it.

For the individual, too, the Creed is a powerful symbol. The promises of faith made at baptism and repeated at confirmation are the reference points of a personal way of life. By their renewal each year at the Easter Vigil we reinforce the importance of this proclamation and recognise that it lies at the foundation of discipleship. It is the kernel around which meaning develops and coherence is to be found. It is who we are and our deepest identity.

Life's Backdrop

Another way of expressing this same point is to speak of the Creed as providing the context in which we live our lives and make our judgements. The Creed can be understood as the backcloth against which all more particular moments are to be seen and issues considered. As every theatre-goer knows, the backcloth is an important part of the play. It not only sets the scene, but it can also shape the viewers' perspectives quite profoundly. A changed backcloth can alter radically the impact and interpretation of the action played out before it. And if this is true in theatre, then it is true in life.

Think, if you will, of a dead tree.[1]Perhaps it has been struck by lightning, or by some deadly disease. It stands, stark and lifeless, the victim of natural disaster, natural evil. It is a symbol of frustrated nature, a sign of much that each of us knows from experience. Natural disasters touch many lives: accidents while travelling, natural disasters of flood and fire, tragedies which are not anyone's fault or the result of sin, but simply the sad effects of a breakdown in the natural order. We all know loved ones in wheelchairs, with walking frames and in the protection of sheltered accommodation. How do we

[1] This image, and analogy, is well presented by WH Vanstone in his book, *Love's Endeavour, Love's Expense*, Darton, Longman and Todd, 1979

live with that? In what perspectives can we view such sadness and frustration?

The dead tree is seen by all as a wasted thing. Yet on occasion the backcloth of the dead tree can change. Set against a vivid sunset it can suddenly become an object of great beauty, its fine tracery etched against the red sky. When covered in frost and set against a sky of winter blue, the dead tree can suddenly reveal its inner beauty, its delicacy and vulnerability. It can literally take our breath away. In such settings, in such perspectives, the tree is endowed with nobility and beauty.

The gift of faith, especially expressed in its key symbols such as the Creed, provides the setting, the perspective, in which we are invited to view not only the joys of life, but also its cruelties and tragedies. The eyes of faith and love can find in frustrated nature a deeper beauty, purpose and nobility. In the light of a more hidden destiny the true worth of the present moment can be seen and appreciated. Symbols of faith work for our redemption because they declare to us the true purposes of so much that might seem not only pointless but tragically cruel. It is for this purpose that we recite, or sing, the Creed.

Creator of All

Even the briefest of reflections on the individual statements, or articles, of the Creed, makes clear this symbolic function. A proclamation of the Father as 'maker of heaven and earth, of all things visible and invisible' gives us our basic orientation towards the created world. In this proclamation we set out the fundamental value which we see in all creation. This is the point from which we start to reflect on issues such as the environment or the treatment of animals. Of itself, this declaration does not resolve the many difficult dilemmas and ambiguities which we encounter. But our basic stance, our gathering point, is made clear.

This phrase of the Creed was one of the favourite 'gathering points' for Pope John Paul II. He used it to great effect in a homily he gave on 8 April 1994. That day saw the unveiling of the restored frescos of Michelangelo in the Sistine Chapel in Rome. Meditating on the way in which Michelangelo had the audacity to portray the Father in the very act of creation, the Pope went on to reflect on the nakedness of the human bodies included in the frescos.

The Sistine Chapel is precisely – if one may say so – the sanctuary of the theology of the human body. In witnessing to the beauty of man created by God as male and female, it also expresses in a certain way the hope of a world transfigured, the world inaugurated by the Risen Christ, and even before by Christ on Mount Tabor.

If we are dazzled as we contemplate the Last Judgement by its splendour and its terror, admiring on the one hand the glorified bodies and on the other those condemned to eternal damnation, we understand too that the whole composition is deeply penetrated by a unique light and by a single artistic logic: the light and the logic of faith that the Church proclaims, confessing: 'I believe in one God... maker of heaven and earth, of all things visible and invisible'. On the basis of this logic in the context of the light that comes from God, the human body also keeps its splendour and its dignity. If it is removed from this dimension, it becomes in some way an object, which depreciates very easily, since only before the eyes of God can the human body remain naked and unclothed and keep its splendour and its beauty intact.

The faith professed in the Creed, then, actually shapes our approach to and feelings for our own bodies. As part of that wonderful creation, we see ourselves, and those whom we love, as clothed in 'splendour and dignity' even without the assistance of fine clothes or formal outfits. Perhaps this also offers a brief reflection on the experience of those whose love is rightly expressed in physical and sexual intimacy. To love another in and with the body is a way of revealing the true beauty of that body when seen with the 'eyes of God', eyes shared to some extent by those who love each other. As we like to say: 'Beauty is in the eye of the beholder'. The invitation of love in marriage is, then, for the spouses to remind each other of the bodily beauty given them by God and to keep fresh the promise of a transformation of that very body, the promised destiny of those who put their trust in God.

Christ Our Lord

The proclamation of the key events of the life, death and resurrection of the Lord spell out the position which Christ occupies in our perceptions and interpretations of life. 'True God from true God', 'through him all things were made'. He is indeed the key to the truth of human experience.

The Pastoral Constitution of the Second Vatican Council spelled this out most powerfully:

It is the Church's belief that Christ, who died and was raised for everyone, offers to the human race through his Spirit, the light and strength to respond to its highest calling; and that no other name under Heaven is given to people for them to be saved. It likewise believes that the key and the focus and culmination of all human history are to be found in its Lord and master. The Church also affirms that underlying so many changes there are some things which do not change and are founded upon Christ, who is the same yesterday and today and forever. It is accordingly in the light of Christ, who is the image of the invisible God and the first-born of all creation, that this council proposes to elucidate the mystery of humankind and, in addressing all people, to contribute to discovering a solution to the outstanding questions of our day (Pastoral Constitution, *Gaudium et Spes*, para 10).

Christ is the 'key', the 'focus', the 'culmination'. He is the ultimate 'symbol', the point and source of meaning and unity for all humanity. Such is our proclamation of faith, week by week.

The Creed also brings us, unequivocally, to the heart of the mystery of Christ, the mystery of God's saving action in our midst. We proclaim:

For our sake he was crucified under Pontius Pilate he suffered death and was buried,...

In this stark statement we confront again the figure of evil, disintegration, suffering and death. Here too, on a different tree, is the image of wasted nature, of futile suffering, before which we are rendered helpless. Unless we grasp this crucial aspect of our symbol of faith, then all our interpretation of life's experience will be wrong. The Christ who is the 'key', the 'focus', the 'culmination' of all human history, is indeed the Christ who hangs helpless on the cross.

One of the most helpful reflections of this dimension of the Gospel is to be found in a book called *The Stature of Waiting* by WH Vanstone. In it he explains how the key moment in the Gospel of Luke is the moment when Judas approaches Jesus in the Garden of Gethsemane and kisses him. This kiss is the moment when the whole shape of the Gospel changes. It lies at the centre of the unfolding Gospel story. This moment, so loved by artists such as Giotto, is like a hinge: the Gospel swings round on it to reveal its deepest secrets.

Vanstone points out that the moment of the kiss of Judas is the moment in which Jesus ceases to be the subject of the Gospel narrative and becomes its object. The verbs describing the actions of Jesus turn from being active to passive. Up to this point, the Gospel narrative tells us what Jesus said and did. Now it becomes a story of what happens to Jesus, what others said about him, and what others did to him. From being the driving force of the Gospel, Jesus now becomes its victim. He is arrested, taken away, put on trial, scourged, executed and buried. All these things must happen to him until, in the phrase of the Gospel, 'it is accomplished'. But when we see this suffering of Christ, his tears, sweat, blood and broken body in the full context of the whole Creed, then we understand that this is precisely the arena of God's saving activity. The helplessness of Christ becomes the revelation and the embodiment of the saving truth. Faith does indeed give the context, the backcloth, against which the hidden meaning of the passivity of Christ is to be read.

It is to the sacramental celebration of that saving truth that the Mass now moves. The Creed is the bridge between the Word and the Eucharist. From the dialogue of one we move to the sacramental action of the other. And we make the transition through our proclamation of this great symbol of faith, a symbol which draws together to a point of profound unity not only our disparate views about the complexities of life, not only our sense of being scattered throughout history, but also that most disintegrating experience of all: the experience of those forces which crush and seemingly destroy our very selves. It is these experiences above all else which we must bring to Christ and to his redemptive sacrifice on the wood of the cross, made present now in the action of the Mass.

Questions for Reflection

1. The Sea of Galilee represents the dark and unknown in life. Jesus came walking on its waters to the disciples. Could you reflect on the moments when the calm presence of Christ has come to you in moments of distress? Was it through another person? Could you share these experiences with others?

2. Have you known someone who lived through a period of suffering with their eyes firmly on the Lord? What difference did this make to their experience? What impact did it have on you?

3. Which phrase of the Creed strikes you most forcefully?

4. Sometimes the Church seems to be pulling itself apart over various disagreements. How can the singing and saying of the Creed help us to see a way beyond these disagreements?

5. Are there other steps you would like to see taken in order to bring out into the open the fundamental unity in faith of members of the Church?

Prayer

Lord our God, nothing is beyond your reach, beyond your healing touch. Help us to look calmly at our fears and distress. Give us the assurance of faith so that in you we may see our lives in the light of your truth. Clinging to you may we not be overwhelmed by panic, bitterness, or exhaustion. Rather, let us see your glory hidden even in the darkest places. We make this prayer through Christ our Lord. Amen.

FIVE
THE WORK OF
HUMAN HANDS

Blessed are you, Lord God of all creation,
for through your goodness we have received
the bread we offer you

Some of my early years as a priest were spent in the south end of Liverpool. One of my abiding memories of that time is of a conversation with a young sociology student from Liverpool University. She was studying patterns of religious observance and behaviour in the neighbourhood. One of her observations was fascinating. She told me that, as she went from door to door asking whether church attendance was part of the inhabitants' pattern of life, she learned that those who did not go to church knew for sure who did. Anyone on the block or street who went regularly to church was known, noted and observed by whose who did not. In fact, she went on, they expressed some irritation and disappointment when, for whatever reason, one of the church-goers gave up the practice!

Now while such sociological patterns may not be widely repeated, they do point to an important point: those who come to church do so on behalf of many others. The Sunday Mass congregation is a gathering of representatives. We are there not simply to pray for ourselves, nor even for the wider circle of our family and friends. Rather, in a very real sense, we are there as a sign of all the people, and we are invited to act, in prayer and worship, on their behalf.

The Prayers of the Faithful are a clear indication of this. Such prayers should range widely in their intentions and scope. They should indeed be universal, without losing their particular and local flavour. At first I thought it strange that it was in an enclosed convent that I heard the best Prayers of the Faithful. There the prayers showed a greater sensitivity to critical events in people's lives, both far and near, than I had ever come across in a parish. But perhaps I should not have been so surprised. Through their life of prayer, and attentive listening, these sisters were fully aware of all that was going on around them. They knew well, too, the Catholic tradition which suggests that two-thirds of our prayer should always be centred on the needs of others.

This truth is deepened and made clearer as we move into the more symbolic part of the Mass, the Eucharistic liturgy. Here we are bringing into our prayer and worship not only an awareness of other people, with all their hopes and anxieties, but also the whole of the created order. The symbols of bread and wine, the basic elements of our Eucharistic action, emerge from, and represent, the very fabric of creation and the stuff of everyday living.

I have always liked to believe the story that it was Pope Paul VI who, at the time of his final study and approval of the Missal of 1969, inserted into the prayers of preparation over the bread and wine the lovely phrase the 'work of human hands'. This might be a tiny phrase, so easily lost in the movement, or the music, of the Offertory, but it is full of resonance.

These words remind us of the full scope of the sacramental action in which we are engaged. They prompt us not to limit, or minimise, the breadth of the reality we are celebrating. They remind us that in taking these elements of bread and wine we are, first and foremost, members of a human family which must earn its sustenance from a resistant earth by toil and ingenuity. These simple words can prevent us from thinking of the Mass simply as an expression of the devotion and prayer of a small group of people. It is so much more. It embraces the whole of our common effort to make our world a place of fruitfulness, order and beauty.

The Whole Created Order

Of course, the bread and the wine represent the unity of the Church. But seen in their wider context they are also symbols of the whole created order which, in Christ, is about to be taken up, refashioned and reborn. This is the vision given by St Paul at the beginning of his Letter to the Church of Colossae. In Christ he sees not simply his personal Lord, nor indeed the leader of the group of disciples. Rather in Christ he sees 'the first-born of all creation, for in him were created all things in heaven and on earth' for 'before anything was created, he existed, and he holds all things in unity.' Then he goes on one more step: 'as he is the Beginning, he was first to be born from the dead, so that he should be first in every way, because God wanted all perfection to be found in him' (Col 1:15-20). The bread and wine placed on the altar, and about to become the real and sacramental presence of the Lord, already speak to us of this deeper meaning of Christ. As 'fruit of the earth and work of human hands' they already point to Christ, the Word of creation and the first- born of the new creation. Our Eucharistic action has cosmic significance.

All this is rather hard to take in. But the prayers are there to help us. They are addressed to 'Lord God of all creation'. They are prayers of blessing, of thanksgiving for all the blessings which we receive:

the gift of life, of goodness, of created beauty, of the satisfaction of purposeful activity, of ingenuity and inventiveness, of the marvels of science and the wonders of outer space. They are prayers and actions by which the whole of that created realm is placed on the altar, and offered to the God in whom they have their origin and, indeed, in whom they will find their fulfilment.

Pope John Paul II, in *Gaudium et spes(2),* expressed it this way:

> It is precisely this world of today that we offer with Christ to the Father in the Holy Spirit, the whole human family, together with the sum of those realities in the midst of which that family lives.

But what is more, these prayers also help us to recognise our own role in that great and cosmic endeavour. It is not the raw forces of nature which are there as our offering. Rather it is the 'work of human hands', our best efforts to shape and fashion that reality, to work with it for the common good. It is every venture by which we have tried to develop the created order, harness its potential for good and draw out its beauty.

A Flawed Gift

Yet so much of that effort is flawed. The scars on the face of the earth bear eloquent testimony to the mistreatment of the created order. Not all has been badly intended: much is the fruit of ignorance. Yet much is deliberate exploitation. The 'work of human hands' is not all a cause of pride. So we bring our failures to the altar, too. For Christ is not only the Word through whom all comes into being, he is also the one in whom the whole of creation will find its fulfilment: the first-born from the dead. In him ecology finds its promise, for in him 'God wanted all perfection to be found and all things to be reconciled through him and for him, everything in heaven and everything on earth' (Col 1:19). The promise of the future glory of creation is held out in the risen Christ, whose mystery we are about to celebrate.

How well I recall the remarks of a mother attending the first Mass celebrated by her son, a newly ordained priest. She said, with wonderful simplicity and insight, 'just think: there's my Frank holding the whole of creation in his hands.' For her, the prayers which we say at the Easter Vigil, proclaiming Christ as the 'Alpha and Omega, the Beginning and the End' of all things, found vivid expression in the Eucharist.

Not everyone sees the richness of Christ with such clarity. But with care and attention we can develop an understanding of Christ as the focal point of all creation and of the Mass as the sacrament of the fulfilment of that created order. In him the work of our human hands finds its true purpose: as a contribution to the re-creation of our world according to the intention of the Creator. In him, too, the work of those same hands, the bread and wine, actually become the substance of his sacramental presence.

Baptismal Calling and Task

We can reflect, for example, on the meaning of our baptism. Through that sacrament we become part of the continuing presence of Christ, the outflow of God's own love at work in our world. This love and power, which we speak of as the Holy Spirit, is in each of the baptised. It is the thrust and energy of our continuing task of bringing the realities of daily life into the ordering and saving sphere of God. Sometimes we speak of the 'priesthood of all the baptised'. This priesthood is, in fact, the first and most fundamental share in the priesthood of Christ. In that priesthood Christ offers, consecrates, all reality to the Father. This is the priesthood in which all the baptised share. Its first and most important task is that of making the world a place marked by awareness and responsiveness to God.

Sometimes, in the Catholic mind, priesthood is to do with the clergy, the church and the altar. The action of

God and the focus of holiness is centred there. Life becomes conveniently separated into the sacred and the secular. The days of the week can be so divided too. The business of the sacred – that search for God, and our response to God – is first and foremost the task of the priest and of Sunday. The lay person's task is to get on with secular living, earn enough to keep body and soul together and, for some, to give support and loyalty to the Church and the clergy in their sacred duties. But such a split won't do. 'The Church by its very nature is immersed in the secular, in the realities of the age.' So said Pope John Paul II at the closing of the 1987 Synod of Bishops on the Vocation and Mission of the Lay Faithful in the Church and in the World. The front line of the Church is the baptised lay people whose first religious tasks and responsibilities are to be the priests of the world, the points at which the love and power of God find flesh in today's realities, and the instruments by which that reality is made holy.

This is no easy task. Daily realities are complex and often bewildering. Who can find a way easily through the jungle of the dole queue, seeking out the signs of God's compassionate love and readily cooperating with them? Who can discern the movement of the Spirit of God in the cut and thrust of boardroom discussions and decisions, and seek wherever possible to take a step in the construction of a more just and fruitful society? It is not easy to be a doctor, health visitor or publican and try to bring wholeness and holiness to everything that is to be done, or to stand against some things which should not. These are no easy tasks, and there are no easy answers. The teachings of the Church recognise this.

> It is to the laity that secular duties and activities belong. When they act as citizens of the world, they will not only be observing the conditions appropriate to each sphere but they will also be acquiring real expertise in those areas. They will willingly cooperate with others who have the same goal. The laity may expect enlightenment and spiritual help from the clergy. But they should not consider that their pastors always have the expertise needed to provide a concrete and ready answer to every problem which arises, even the most serious ones, or that this is their mission. The laity, as enlightened with Christian wisdom and paying careful attention to the teaching of the magisterium, have their own part to play. (Pastoral Constitution, *Gaudium et Spes*, para 43).

Leadership in the Church

Clearly, an important and consistent task required of the Church is to assist people in this struggle to sanctify everyday living. History demonstrates that the clergy are not always best in tune with the task. Major lessons illustrate this. The broad aims of 'liberty, equality and fraternity', which lay at the heart of the French Revolution, were only accepted in their fullness by the leadership of the Church one hundred years after the period of revolution had ended. Of course, these aims were deeply obscured by the complexity of the historical situation and the various alignments between the ruling bodies and the Church. It is also true that such values had a more remote origin in the traditions of Catholic philosophy. Yet their formal recognition by the Church was slow in coming. The prominent part they now play in current Church teaching is bound up with the vision and sacrifice hidden in that social revolution.

In a similar manner, and nearer to our day, commentators on the emergence of the Solidarity movement in Poland, leading up to the fall of Soviet domination, point out that the full support of the hierarchy of the Church was not in evidence in its early days. Clearly, under the leadership of Pope John Paul II, that support became strong and, in all probability, decisive. But it took some time for the true nature and potential of the movement to be recognised by the hierarchy and for the risks involved to be accepted. These are salutary reminders that it is a mistake for bishops, priests or lay leaders in the Church to seek to dominate or direct an assessment of movements in society. Such assessment is complex and needs the careful contribution of many perspectives, and not a little time.

The task of leadership in the Church, then, is often to listen attentively to the accounts of social movement, whether national or local, and assist in the process of discernment. Here, perhaps, a familiarity with the Scriptures is an essential contribution. Familiarity with the patterns of the gospel stories should enable leaders to recognise those same patterns beginning to emerge in any particular situation. The task is to become aware of the presence of God at work in the world, even in the most unexpected places.

A second quality required of those in leadership in the Church is honesty in the accounts given of how things are in the world. It is so easy for clergy to lose a full and critical view of daily living. Perhaps this comes out in alternative extremes. There are those whose view of life is dominated by 'doom and gloom'. Over and over they will be heard decrying modern society, listing its ills, emphasising its failures. It is done with the best of intentions: that of calling people back to the teachings of the Lord. In contrast, there are those whose preaching never seems to get beyond the point of affirming the goodness of God and the inherent goodness of the created order. Some even have badges to illustrate it! Yet neither approach serves the difficult task of coming to understand the presence of God in our world, respond to it, and cooperate in God's work. Unrealistic assessments, especially when presented from the pulpit, serve only to strengthen the sense that 'the Church' is distant from everyday life. In contrast we need a recognition of the fact that in this present age both 'wheat' and 'tares' are growing side by side. Our task is that of a careful discernment in which there will normally be no plainly obvious right course of action but a recognition of the ambiguities of most situations. This sensitivity is not an excuse for inaction, but it is a counter-balance to uncritical enthusiasms which often seek to reduce the Gospel message to a single political slogan or programme for action.

Fashioning a Worthy Offering

Yet even more crucial, in my view, is the task of helping people to bring to God their own personal efforts as a 'worthy offering'. This task underlies the moment of the Mass which we are considering, the presentation of the gifts. But it can also be seen in other moments in the Church's liturgy and sacramental practice. May I illustrate this with reference to the sacrament of confirmation.

For many reasons confirmation is a powerful and deeply felt moment. As well as having powerful social dimensions, confirmation is, in my experience at least, also an important moment in the life of faith of the youngsters involved. They attend weeks of preparation; they go away on retreat, probably for the first time in their lives; they form bonds of friendship in the context of exploring faith together; they genuinely prepare for that moment when, in front of a full church, they profess their own personal faith. For the parents, too, this is a remarkable moment. Their child, so long utterly dependent on them, now stands in her or his own right, apart from them, and speaks out. It is not surprising that in most cases new clothes are bought for the occasion: clothes chosen by the youngster, yet paid for by the parents! In the ceremony itself the fruit of years of great effort, discipline and sacrifice, especially on the part of parents, can be seen standing there in the benches of the church.

Obviously not all is just as the parents, or the youngsters themselves, might wish. Some are ungainly and self-conscious, others just too sophisticated for their years; some are on the verge of rebellion, others full of studied indifference. Yet all are there, supported by their families and peer group. Here, indeed, is the 'work of human hands'. In this sacrament, in a particularly direct way, that work is presented to God, celebrated by the community, received by the Church in the person of the bishop, and consecrated, or given a new 'order', in the life and mission of the Church.

Small Signs of God's Presence

This, I hope, illustrates the more central task of the Church: to help people to bring the work of their hands to the altar as a worthy offering. If this is to be done, week after week, then we must start by recognising God's presence in the effort which each person makes, day by day. A walk around many a suburban estate illustrates this point. Garden after garden speaks of the daily effort that the householders have made: tended hedges, neat borders, flowers in bloom. Such effort is an expression of care, not just for the plants and flowers, but also for the environment in which daily life is carried out. Care for a garden is an expression of love by the people of the house, a steadfast love that sustains the work week by week, in each different season. So the garden is a sign of the deeper care with which so many people seek to support each other, in good times and bad, in family and friendship. This steadfast loving is shot through with the presence of God. It is sometimes an eloquent parable of that presence of God. When that presence of God is recognised, then the desire to thank God begins to take root and become the motive for prayer and participation in the liturgy of the Church. In fact, that recognition of the presence of a giver in our lives, often half-formed or only dimly perceived, leads to the instinct or desire to 'go to church', at least for special occasions or needs. There people seek reassurance of God's abiding presence and seek the blessings, the bounty, of the giver of all gifts.

It is surely at the heart of the mission of the Church to shape that response into a worthy offering. From a point of such half-realisation, we need to progress in awareness and response to a point at which we are consciously offering every aspect of our daily lives to the Father, and consciously trying to live it in a way that is pleasing to him. Perhaps this is the lesson of the parable of the widow's mite in St Luke's Gospel (21:1-4). Alone among all those making their offerings, the widow has come to an understanding that, at root, everything is a gift of God and, therefore, everything she has can be freely offered to God in return.

Getting It Right

The disciplines of the Church are some of the ways in which an offering is shaped so that it may become 'worthy'. Traditions of daily prayer and devotions help to centre a life on the will of God; observance of the seasons, particularly the penitential season of Lent, introduce a daily awareness of our dependence on God, especially for forgiveness; attendance at Mass brings the life of faith to its explicit high point, in which our broken gifts become worthy because they are taken up into the one and only worthy offering, that of Christ himself. The use of symbols and rituals, as given in the rites of the Church, are an important part of the fashioning of a worthy offering. Perhaps this awareness lies at the root of the instinct of so many Catholics that the liturgy should be carried out according to the requirements of the Church. 'Do it properly, Father' is a comment that I hear every now and then; more often I receive complaints that it is not done so. This is more than ritualism. It is, perhaps, a realisation that the giving of a gift needs more than spontaneity. It needs costly discipline, not only in the fashioning of the gift, but also in the manner of its presentation. Such costly discipline is willingly given by love.

Some would say that the construction and care of the church building is also an important demonstration of this discipline of love, the fashioning of an offering made out of the fabric of our lives and the work of human hands. It is certainly true that a parish involved in the construction of a new church finds a depth of willing sacrifice that is always surprising. The church building itself, so soon to be a place of prayer, praise and peace, is a most powerful symbol of God's presence in the hustle and bustle of daily life. It will be the focal point of so much joy and hope, sadness and grief, a true embodiment of the pilgrim people in their relationship to God. Its construction, therefore, touches the deepest instincts of faith. So too the maintaining of that property can be a costly discipline of love. In the work of keeping the church clean and beautiful, or dry and watertight, we are fashioning a worthy offering, the work of human hands. All involved in that work may do it explicitly as a prayer to the glory of God and as an expression of their baptismal calling. There are other words, too, in this part of the Mass which are vital if we are to understand this offering of our gift, the work of human hands. Yet these words are not often heard, being either said silently or accompanied by singing. They are words which direct us to the right disposition of heart. If this is lacking, then our offering lacks an essential quality. These words remind us, yet again, that the work in which we are engaged depends totally on God, on God's initiative and forgiveness. The part we play is given only by God's gracious invitation. Our hearts bow low, even as we present our gifts, and we say the words:

> With humble spirit and contrite heart may we be accepted by you, O Lord, and may our sacrifice in your sight this day be pleasing to you, Lord God.

There is, I believe, great pastoral skill involved in gathering together the offerings of the congregation. We come to church preoccupied with so many things, and yet only one is important. To enable people to bring all their efforts and preoccupations to the Lord, not laying them aside as irrelevant or unworthy, is to unpack the symbolism of the bread and the wine. In doing so we reach out beyond ourselves and draw onto the altar much human endeavour. Then we come to see more clearly the wider movement and meaning of the Mass itself.

Questions for Reflection

1. In what way is your daily effort directed at giving shape and order to this world? Where do you feel that chaos is creeping in? Can you bring this work of your hands and make it part of your prayer at Mass?

2. In what ways have you ever sensed the 'cosmic' meaning of the Mass? Do you know what the mother of the new priest mentioned in this chapter was getting at?

3. What do you understand by the 'priesthood of all the baptized'? Does it seem to be taking something away from the ordained priesthood? Can you think together about how these two are related to each other and, in fact, depend on each other?

4. In your opinion, what are the movements in society that have been closer to the gospel than the position of the church as formally expressed? Why do you think this might have been the case?

5. Are there any times and occasions when you have sensed in others a vague desire to 'go to church'? Have you been able to build on this? Could you do so?

Prayer

Lord our God, we thank you for the gift of our world, with all its beauty and grandeur. Help us to be careful stewards of your creation. Guide with your wisdom our ingenuity and enterprise so that we may enhance creation by our efforts. Help us to fashion of our lives a worthy offering so that we may come at last to the promise of our future glory, when all will be fulfilled in your splendour. We make this prayer through Christ our Lord. Amen.

SIX

THE DIVINE
AND THE HUMAN

Through him, and with him and in him, O God,
almighty Father, in the unity of the Holy Spirit,
all glory and honour is yours, for ever and ever.

The best known of all the words written by St Augustine must be those in which he speaks of the restlessness of our hearts finding satisfaction only in God. The very popularity of the saying tells us that it corresponds to the experience of many. In fact there is a strong strand in our spiritual tradition that seeks to explain much of religious experience precisely in terms of a constant search for God, driven by a restless heart seeking its ultimate fulfilment.

But another strand exists, too. This alternative version stresses that the whole of religious experience consists not so much in our search for God, as in God's search for us. The scriptural basis for this version is strong indeed. From the very opening lines and construction of the Book of Genesis, the implication is clearly that it is God who not only calls all life into existence, but who wants to delight in that life as much as possible. In fact, it can be reasonably claimed that the one story running throughout the Scriptures is that of God's search for us. Joseph is cast into the well by his brothers, and yet brought out again to be sold into slavery (Gen 38); Moses is sought out and rescued from the certainty of death, both as a male Jew and from the perils of the river (Exod 1 and 2); Zaccheus is brought down from his sycamore tree at the invitation of the Lord (Luke 19). Over and over again, as Eucharistic Prayer IV says so clearly, God offers a new agreement, a new covenant to us, inviting us to hear and respond. The story of faith is certainly a story of God's call, God's search, and of our response to it; or lack of response.

One of the most attractive insights of Ignatian spirituality is that in every circumstance God is there, coming to meet us. God is present in our sickness and in our health; coming to meet us in friendships and love, both those which 'flow' easily and those which demand great constancy; coming to meet us in difficulties and in joys; coming to meet us, indeed, in the invitation of death itself. The spiritual quest, as understood by St Ignatius, is that of achieving a 'free heart', unencumbered by preoccupations, with which to recognise and welcome the Lord who is always coming to meet us.

The Gift of Love

Whenever we speak of the Church as koinonia or communion we point first to God's invitation to us to share fully in the very life of God. In fact this 'communion of life with God' is the only basis and source of the communion of life we strive to achieve and express in the Church. The Church, as a communion in the life of God, is the sacrament of all that God intends for the whole created order: the kingdom, rooted in God, in which justice, love and peace reign supreme, and in which the unity of the human family is at last fulfilled. This communion of life is nothing other than the gift of love.

Yet here we come to a paradox. The exchange of gifts requires an appreciation of the capacity of the recipient for the intended gift. It is rather pointless to give a child an adult gift, unless it is meant to be left in the cupboard. Furthermore, the gift of a sharing of life, given in love, implies a judgement that there is sufficient equality between giver and receiver for that sharing of life to be meaningful. There must be a certain equality between those who seek to share in one common life. Certainly this capacity may not be in a state of full realisation. But nobody can give the gift of love, in a healthy and mature way, to another who does not have the capacity to receive and respond to it.

There are, of course, many kinds of love, some of which fall far short of this paradigm. In fact, some experiences are only spoken of as love by a kind of analogy. I think we speak only loosely of people loving their pet animals. There are other forms of 'love', too, which are distortions, immature or imperfect. Excessive dependence on a friend, spouse, parent or religious superior may look like steadfast devotion but can be quite unhealthy. Sometimes a bonding between two people, spoken of as love, can become so obsessive that it slowly but steadily destroys them both. On the other hand, parents who love their children want them to grow to mature adulthood and not stay as dependent children. Mature, adult love, in its fullness, strives to be a communion of equals. That is why it is so hard to achieve.

So the dilemma we face in reflecting on the invitation of God to share the gift of life in its fullness is that there is simply no possible equality between giver and receiver. We are, quite simply, creatures. God, quite simply, is the Creator. Here is an unbridgeable gap. Logically, the consequence of this is that the relationship between God and ourselves is either not thoroughly love in the proper sense of the word, or not unequivocally with God.

An instinctive awareness of this problem may lie at the root of distortions in our relationship with God. Not infrequently this relationship is cast in terms that

are not those of mature and fruitful love. At times we turn to God in our helplessness for protection. We want a protective parent. Similarly, we may turn to God for mercy and forgiveness only when we feel a sense of hopelessness in ourselves. Then we seek out the one on to whom we can cast our burdens, escaping from those things which of themselves will crush us. While there is truth in both of these relationships, neither is an expression of that full communion of life spoken of in our doctrine.

The alternative way of accommodation is to reduce our understanding of God so that the giver of all gifts is brought down to our level and spoken of in terms which are purely human. Such a god is indeed accepted as a presence in our lives, but more as a rather special actor or arranger of events than as the source of all life. This is a god who stands on our stage, mighty in proportion but still, fundamentally, within our range, though frustratingly often uncooperative. Similarly our religious experience can be miscast simply as a relationship with a rather special man, Jesus of Nazareth, who showed us how to live and how to die generously for others.

Called to be Divine

The teaching of our faith is not to be found in any of these reduced versions. They lose the full drama of the truth. Rather, we are called into a full relationship of life and love with the God who alone is the source and origin of all. In other words, we are called to be divine. There is no other way of putting it. There is no other way of holding together the implications of this invitation. Only God could issue such an invitation, and only God bring it to pass.

This indeed is the Gospel call. Again and again the Gospel speaks to us of God 'coming to make his home with us'. Such is the Father's love that nothing less seems to suffice: he wants to draw us into intimacy with himself. Only the language of home and hearth will do.

This same truth is spelt out for us in a dramatic way in a prayer in the Mass which so often goes unnoticed. As the priest mixes a drop of water with the wine, during the preparation of the gifts, he says these remarkable words:

> By the mystery of this water and wine may we come to share in the divinity of Christ who humbled himself to share in our humanity.

And there we have it. We are called to share in the divine life itself. The invitation, issued fully in the person of Jesus, is achieved in him through the power of the Holy Spirit. By our union with Christ, through baptism, through prayer, through the action of the Mass, we are being taken into the heart of the life of the Trinity itself: that exchange of life and love between Father, Son and Holy Spirit. This, then, becomes our dwelling place, our true home. In the present age it is achieved through the action of the Spirit in the sacramental life, but in the time to come it will be experienced face to face.

In considering this remarkable truth, it is important to remember that the essential difference and distance between God and us is not caused by sin. It is not our sinfulness that creates the gap, for even if we were without all sin we should still be creatures, and God still the Creator. So even if we wished, of ourselves we are not able to take up this invitation. This is spelt out quite unequivocally to Moses:

> 'I have compassion on whom I will, and I show pity to whom I please. You cannot see my face,' Yahweh said 'for man cannot see me and live.' And Yahweh said, 'Here is a place beside me. You must stand on the rock, and when my glory passes by, I will put you in a cleft of the rock and shield you with my hand while I pass by. Then I will take my hand away and you shall see the back of me; but my face is not to be seen' (Exod 33:19-23).

This gap between us and God can only be bridged by God. God does so, in a decisive manner, in the Incarnation of the Eternal Word.

The Longing of God

The Incarnation is, of course, the ultimate expression of that eternal flow of love which is God: love that gives rise to all life, love that now encloses itself in our flesh so that we may be drawn more fully into love's embrace. For this is God's most ardent desire, if we may speak in those terms. The Book of Genesis has already suggested that, in the evening, God came to the Garden seeking out the company of Adam and Eve (cf Gen 3:8). The Song of Songs picks up this theme of God's longing for us and expresses it with such intense passion and longing:

> I went down to the nut orchard to see what was sprouting in the valley, to see if the vines were budding and the pomegranate trees in flower. Before I knew…. My desire had hurled me on the chariots of my people, as prince (S of S 6:11-12).

These words of the Bridegroom disclose the depth of love behind the coming of our Saviour. They cast light on the more measured phrase of St John: 'God so loved the world that he gave his only Son' (John 3:16). The impulse of pure love, burning desire, drives on the whole mystery of salvation: the Father reaching out to his beloved creation, the Son willingly obedient in his gift of self, the Spirit bringing to fruition the love and will of them both.

The working out of God's invitation centres upon the Incarnate Word. The perfect expression not only of the invitation of God but also of the response of the human person can be found only in him who alone is both truly God and fully human. In Jesus Christ alone is the invitation both given and received. In him alone is there both equality with the Father and, within the human family, the capacity and freedom with which to respond in full measure.

This profound and powerful drama of love given, received and returned, is played out, in its fullness in only one place: on the cross at Calvary. The crucifixion of Our Lord is the fullest expression not only of God's love for us but also of the human person's complete response. The crucifixion is the inevitable consequence of the incarnation of the total love of God, seeking us out. Such is the condition of our 'fallen world' that the full embodiment of love could only be rejected. It is simply too much, too shocking for us to embrace. Such is our habitual sinfulness that the total response to such love by Christ could cost nothing less than the breaking of every bone and sinew. Whenever we look at a crucifix we do well to remind ourselves that this is what happens when the fullness of love takes flesh in our sinful world. Such love is misunderstood, exploited and eventually rejected. The meaning of the obedience of the Son, then, is not a submission to a capricious master who has thought up a rather gruesome scenario, but his readiness to be totally and unequivocally true to himself. Eternal Love made flesh, given and answered, costs all.

Christ Our Way

The sign of eternal sonship, then, is the sign of the crucified Lord. There the total love of God is offered and accepted in all its majesty. In the crucified there is no holding back. Love is given by the Godhead. Love is accepted in the flesh. Love is returned in loving obedience. There, in the crucifix, is the fullness of this mystery of the invitation to a 'communion of life'. Jesus, in that moment, reveals that the love of God knows no limits. In that same moment, on behalf of the whole of creation, he responds with total love, casting himself totally on the Father.

At that very moment Jesus is the full expression of Christian prayer. He is the full expression of our relationship to the Father. He is the icon of the 'communion of life', held in suspense, revealing all.

Is it surprising that St Paul often proclaims that he has no life except with Christ, and with him crucified? In the action of the Mass we are drawn into this one crucial event. Only this moment of total revelation, of total obedience, radically changes all our possibilities. Not only is the gap between creature and Creator for ever bridged, for God has embraced our broken human condition, but our capacity to respond has been revealed and released. Without this moment we cannot really live. Without it we can never be truly human, locked forever in the frustration of a longing heart that cannot reach the home for which it has been made. Here, in Christ, is our salvation.

The response of the Father to this total love of the Son is also inevitable, in the sense that it follows from the nature of God. The outpouring of love in Christ's life and death is brought to fulfilment by the power of that same love, the Holy Spirit, in the resurrection of Christ from the dead. The crucified Christ is the fullness of human prayer. His resurrection is the fullness of God's response. Crucifixion and resurrection: prayer and response. If the crucifixion of the Lord is, as it were, the projection into history of the love of God, then the resurrection of the Lord is the projection into history of the power of the Spirit. It is, after all, the same Spirit that 'hovered over the waters', over the 'void', over the 'darkness', effecting the creating will of the Father (Gen 1:1). The same Spirit continues that work, in an unbroken fashion, in the resurrection of the Lord.

Eucharistic Prayer

Each Eucharistic prayer opens with a prayer of praise and thanksgiving; and each comes to the point of its solemn request:

...bless, acknowledge, and approve this offering..., so that it may become for us the Body and Blood of your most beloved Son, our Lord Jesus Christ (Eucharistic Prayer I). Make holy, therefore, these gifts, we pray, by sending down your Spirit upon them like the dewfall, so that they may become for us the Body and Blood of our Lord, Jesus Christ (Eucharistic Prayer II).

The prayer then changes. It recognizes that the decisive intervention of the power of God, the Holy Spirit, was in the person of Jesus Christ, in the events of his life, death, and resurrection. The prayer, therefore, tells again those events, and through the priest, whom the Spirit uses as an instrument, the words of Christ are filled with life, and bread and wine become exactly what the words proclaim.

The Eucharistic Prayer then returns to its opening style. Now the whole Church prays through the priest, who stretches out his arms, in a reflection of the crucified Lord. For it is indeed Christ who prays. Christ is present, in the offering now on the altar, and it is he who beseeches the Father for the well-being of the Church, for the living and the dead, for the salvation of the whole world. The Son, on our behalf, addresses the Father in the power and love of the Holy Spirit.

So when, in the prayer of the Mass, we stand with Christ at the event of his crucifixion and resurrection, we are taken up into the very heart of God and into the gift of the communion of life. Christ, the Incarnate Word, through whom all things were made, contains within himself the whole of humanity, the whole of the created order. In him all is lifted to the Father in that one act of love. Christ is our prayer. He is all prayer. In this sense, there can be no prayer except through him, for he alone is the spoken Word of God and the 'spoken' response of the created order.

This is the stunning vision offered by Pope John Paul II as he invited us to prepare for the advent of the third millennium. Perhaps the most important part of his message was its first seven pages, in which he reflected on the Word of God, Jesus Christ. He said:

> In Christ all things come into their own; they are taken up and given back to the Creator from whom they first came (*Tertio Millennio Adveniente* para 6).

He then expressed the startling and at times disturbing claim of the Christian faith:

> Christ is thus the fulfilment of the yearning of all the world's religions and, as such, he is their sole and definitive completion. Just as God in Christ speaks to humanity of himself, so in

Christ all humanity and the whole of creation speaks of itself to God – indeed it gives itself to God (para 6).

These reflections find a dramatic expression in a central moment of the celebration of Mass, a moment which, for me, is indeed a climax. At the conclusion of the Eucharistic Prayer, the priest raises the body and blood of the Lord saying:

Through him, and with him and in him, O God, almighty Father, in the unity of the Holy Spirit, all glory and honour is yours, for ever and ever.

And the whole people, on behalf of the created order, respond: Amen, It is so, Amen. In these words we profess that the one and only prayer is Christ; the only possibility of human prayer is in him; the perfect prayer is him. In, through and with him we pray at this moment and always.

Perfect Prayer

It is important to remember that this lifting of the body and blood of the Lord is not a showing of them to the people, as happens after the consecration or just before the sharing of Holy Communion. This, rather, is a lifting of the Son to the Father, in a sublime act of priesthood, the priesthood of

Christ embodied in the ordained minister. It is the moment in which the shape of our salvation is again revealed and its saving power made present. In him prayer becomes possible, no longer requiring futile sacrifices or superstitions. In him prayer is perfect and complete. We are drawn into the very life of the Trinity: the Son perfectly expressing the love and will of the Father, the Father bestowing on the Son the fullness of life; the Spirit bringing it all about. Without him we are creatures, unable truly to address God. With him we are made whole and partners in the divine enterprise. Or, as Pope John Paul II has said:

> In Jesus Christ, God not only speaks to every person but also seeks out him (or her)... He does so because he loves every person eternally in Christ and wishes to raise every human being to the dignity of an adoptive son... to share in the inmost life of God (*Tertio Millennio Adveniente*, paras 7 and 8).

These are some of the thoughts that fill my mind at this moment of the Mass. It brings into the present the drama of the words of St John's Gospel:

> No one has gone up to heaven
> except the one who came down from heaven,
> the Son of Man who is in heaven;
> and the Son of Man must be lifted up

as Moses lifted up the serpent in the desert,
so that everyone who believes
may have eternal life in him
(John 3:13).

At this moment we are caught up in the one event which lies at the centre of human history. Prefigured in so many ways in the Old Testament, it took place on Calvary, and is now continued in the sacramental life of the Church. It can be summarised in these lovely words:

As our priest, Christ prays for us; as our head, he prays in us; as our God, we pray to him, but let us recognise our voices in him and his voice in us (Liturgy of the Hours, Responses, Vol 1, p 439).

The practical implications of this mystery are, of course, many. How well I remember, in the reordering of one parish church, the insistence of a young priest that a large crucifix, which was being moved from a high central position, be placed within reach of the people. Now, with a kneeler at its foot, it has become a point of daily devotion. The feet of the figure of Christ are being worn smooth by the touches and kisses of many. The instinct of faith knows its source of life.

In like manner, I always find the Adoration of the Cross in the Liturgy of Good Friday a moving occasion. With great patience and deep devotion, huge congregations wait for the moment when each can come to the cross and kiss its saving wood, or indeed, the feet of the figure of Christ. This surely is a moment which ought not to be rushed, or ever over organised simply for efficiency.

It is good to remember, too, that much is to be learned from the faith of those who, in their daily living, stand nearest to the cross of Christ. The poor, the broken, the oppressed, the sick and the dying share in a particular way in the self-offering of the Son to the Father and in the 'work' of our salvation. Their offering continues to be made in and through the body of Christ. It is completed only when all has been returned to the Father and all is made whole. In Christ, through him and with him the one sacrifice of Calvary continues, for the eternal Word is still spoken, his incarnate body still offered to the Father, and the work of the Holy Spirit continues unabated.

When we lift up again the body and blood of Christ, be it in the smallest chapel or greatest cathedral, we lift up all human striving, all humanity's attempts to 'get it right'. Our efforts at human loving, at good government, at industrial or academic excellence, all are included. And in that moment, in our total incorporation into Christ, all finds its fulfilment. In him it is achieved, accomplished. In us it is, as yet, still a promise.

Questions for Reflection

1. What is the greatest gift you have ever received? In what way did it 'fit' you, so that you could not only receive but also respond to it?

2. What are the ways in which you are tempted to distort your relationships with God? Does God provide only protection or escape from life? Or has God become a very powerful 'actor' in your world who sometimes, inexplicably, seems to let you down?

3. Our life can be understood as a preparation for that moment of perfection when we shall see God face to face, when 'we shall be like him'. Are there any ways in which this thought helps you to understand our journey through life?

4. The Mass can be experienced as a making real of the moment of the Last Supper, or the moment of our Lord's death on the cross. Do either of these images help you? If so, why? Are there other images that help you to understand the Mass?

5. Do you have a crucifix at home? Where does it hang? When you look at it, what do you think, or pray?

Prayer

Lord our God, your Son died for us on the cross of Calvary. Help us to see in that event the source of our salvation. Help us to cling to Christ so that he may bring us to you, for that is your burning desire. Pour into our hearts the gift of the Holy Spirit that we may not only receive the gift of your life but also respond to it with all our hearts. We make this prayer through Christ our Lord. Amen.

SEVEN
THE BLOOD OF THE LAMB

*Behold the Lamb of God, behold him who
takes away the sins of the world. Blessed are
those called to the supper of the Lamb.*

A
s the great prayer of Christ to his Father, the
prayer of the Mass, comes to its climax, we
are already beginning to prepare to receive
the Lord in Holy Communion. We have united
ourselves with him in this prayer, and now he gives
himself to us as our food and drink. In preparation
for that moment we pray our family prayer, the words
that he himself gave us. Then, in another moment
of great solemnity, Christ is held before us, for our
adoration, as '...the Lamb of God,... who takes away
the sins of the world'.

The reality of sin is never far away. In fact, most
news bulletins contain items of tragic wrongdoing
which both horrify and fascinate us. Sometimes
it can seem as if the roll-call of such events is
becoming longer and more persistent. Names such
as Enniskillen, Dunblane and '9/11' readily call to

mind the horrors of bomb and bullet, quite apart from wholescale wars. As an instrument of evil, the knife, too, is not far behind. And so are the tongue and pen, even if their evil is more subtle and outwardly respectable. Yet most of us experience the destructiveness of evil in hidden ways, behind family walls, or even more deeply in the recesses of the heart. Every experience of evil summons up one of the most difficult and taxing questions which face us, both individually and as a society. How are we to respond to such experiences? Are we to seek revenge, particularly when we know that the evil cannot be undone? Or are we to try to forgive, even when the wrongdoing has cost us so dearly in terms of life, well-being or peace?

For a Christian the answer to that question may seem self-evident. Indeed we are to forgive those who wrong us, just as we ourselves are forgiven by God. But these words can slip off the tongue far too easily and fail to express the depth and demands which they contain. Many would say that we have both preached and attempted to practice a form of easy forgiveness: sin wiped away with the wave of a hand, with insufficient regard for the damage caused by our sin and the hurt inflicted upon others.

It is not too surprising, then, when secular critics challenge such a notion of 'easy forgiveness' as failing to address the deepest human reality of sin:

the hurt done and the aching wounds left in the minds or hearts of others. Some would argue that these effects are permanent, and the only response to them is to close off that area of life: a failed marriage, hostile neighbours, vengeful acquaintances. In such circumstances human wisdom simply says, 'Stay away'. To preach forgiveness may sound inspiring but perhaps it is not only idealistic but, more worryingly, unattainable.

Costly Forgiveness

Criticisms such as these invite us to look more closely at the reality of forgiveness. Can we really expect the father of a murdered youngster to come to a profound forgiveness of the killers? Or should a person abused in their childhood be encouraged to forgive the perpetrator and simply put the incidents behind them? Not only are such pathways immensely difficult, many would say that they risk seriously compounding the trauma already suffered.

In fact, the way towards eventual forgiveness is long and costly. It is marked by various stages: slowly coming to terms with what has happened, beginning to sense and recover a capacity for life, and gradually gaining some healing. Then, and only then, a person might be able to face and begin to understand the perpetrator. At this point the possibility of offering forgiveness from the heart might begin to emerge. If such steps are most clearly understood in the experiences of profound evil, I think they can be recognised even in lesser matters too: the small betrayal, the lie of convenience, the sudden explosion of a passing rage. Each time we have to work our way through a process such as this in order to find peace and the possibility of forgiveness.

Looked at through the eyes of faith, forgiveness is first of all a gift of God, something that is indeed beyond our own resources. Forgiveness of our sins is not an act by which God overlooks what we have done. Nor does God excuse us, pretending that the offence never took place. Rather, forgiveness is the free gift of being pardoned in such a way that the guilt of the offence is no longer held against the sinner, and in the sight of God its evil effects are replaced by the offer of God-given peace and grace.

The image of the prodigal son (Luke 15:11 ff), so well expressed in the Rembrandt picture, captures much of the inner nature of this gift. So too, I think, do the photographs of Pope John Paul II visiting Ali Agca, his would-be assassin, in the prison cell. The embrace with which the two men parted was far more than a clever photo-call. It was, I believe, a moment of profound forgiveness.

As such images make clear, in order for such a gift to be received, the sinner must be able to acknowledge the sin and turn to God asking for this pardon. Repentance is part of the path of forgiveness. Repentance, like forgiveness, does not involve pretending that the offence never took place, or that it doesn't really matter and can simply be forgotten. In fact, repentance is just the opposite. It involves a deeper realisation of the effects of sin, the damage which has been done, the betrayal involved. Repentance means looking sin in the face and acknowledging its full force. In repentance and forgiveness, nothing is forgotten, nothing is ignored, nothing is easy.

The cost of forgiveness is spelt out most clearly in its central icon: the figure of Christ dying on the cross. In his sweat, in his tears, in his broken body we see the real costliness of the forgiveness of sin. Only by coming to a deeper understanding of the mystery of the cross can we hope to grasp the immensity of the gift of forgiveness. Then we begin to glimpse the true nature of the invitation extended to us so that we too can forgive one another.

Forgiveness and Retaliation

A number of aspects of forgiveness become clearer when we look more closely at the death of Christ. In the first place, the Gospel presentations of the events surrounding the death of Christ bring to the fore the fact that Jesus did not retaliate. He was taken, by force. He was betrayed by one who loved him. He was stripped and publicly humiliated. He was tortured, quite gratuitously. He was put to death, an outcast and an object of scorn. But he did not retaliate. He was indeed a victim and yet he accepted what was happening. He embraced it. But nor did he passively collude. Rather, he recognised in the events the pattern of a different reality: 'the hour for him to pass from this world to the Father' (John 13:1). In doing so, Jesus discloses one of the inner secrets of forgiveness. It can only be achieved when the vicious cycle of oppression and victimisation is broken. Most evil is part of such a cycle. Jesus breaks that vicious dynamic which lies at the heart of evil in our world. His death on the cross is, as it were, a sponge soaking up all the anger that burns in our human hearts and fuels that awful cycle of destruction.

For our part we are mostly caught in this cycle. When we sense we have been victimised, or when we know it for sure, our first and strongest instinct is to turn the tables. We want to rescue ourselves from being the object of anger, deceit, mockery or suffering. We ask ourselves, 'Why is this happening to me? What have I done to deserve this? Why am I its victim?' Then we try hard to draw the other into the line of fire, so that he or she can become the object of the judgement, condemnation and anger of others: a victim in his or her turn.

Of course, the cycles of victimisation and oppression are often more subtle and devious than that. For so is the human heart. Often we face the temptation of playing or exaggerating the role of victim in order to accentuate the guilt to be felt by the other. Sometimes we use our position as victim precisely to oppress another, becoming in our turn a perpetrator of hurt, in the name of retribution or even justice. Revenge is a powerful motive, and it takes on many disguises.

Yet in Christ we have the one who is pure victim. Not only does he embrace his destiny, he consciously turns down means of avoidance and revenge: the sword of his companion Peter (John 18:10) or the plea of innocence (John 19:10). He is indeed the spotless victim. Only when Jesus prays 'Father, forgive them, they do not know what they are doing' (Luke 23:34) is the grip of evil broken. For this reason, we sing in his praise 'O saving victim' and we recognise that forgiveness comes to us only in and through his name.

Forgiveness and the Victim

Even after his resurrection, Jesus comes to us bearing the marks of suffering in his hands, his feet and his side. He is still the victim. And still he refuses to condemn, or in any other way open up again the cycle of retribution. Perhaps this is most clearly shown in his appearance to the disciples on the shores of Lake Tiberias. The disciples catch a glimpse of him standing on the shore. Peter, as impetuous as ever, jumps into the water in his haste to get to the Lord. But when they reach him, they find him standing over a charcoal fire preparing breakfast. For Peter it must have been a devastating moment. Only days earlier he had stood beside another charcoal fire and disowned the Lord three times (John 18:18, 25). That moment must have come flooding back into his mind. Yet the Lord offers no rebuke, no turning of the tables. Instead he offers food. When the food is finished he simply asks Peter, 'Simon, son of John, do you love me?' And he asks it three times. Here, in vivid terms, the cycle of victim and oppressor is broken. Peter is set free, not only to confess his love but also to prepare for his life's mission and indeed his death.

So the paradox of forgiveness is that it is granted through the victim. The wounded Christ is the source of forgiveness. He, the one in whom all things come to be and in whom all things are contained, bears the suffering of us all for he is also the victim in us all. As such he is able to open to all the gift of healing and forgiveness. The Letter of St Peter expresses this succinctly:

> He had not done anything wrong, and there had been no perjury in his mouth. He was insulted and did not retaliate with insults; when

he was tortured he made no threats but he put his trust in the righteous judge. He was bearing our faults in his own body on the cross, so that we might die to our faults and live for holiness: through his wounds you have been healed (1 Pet 2:23-24).

Acknowledging the name of Christ the victim is important, then, because to do so identifies the source of the forgiveness. And this is true in our human quest, too. Part of the search for repentance and forgiveness is a readiness to name both the evil done and the victim who has been hurt, even if the statements are tinged with ambiguity and the possibility of excuses and escapes. In both Church and society forgiveness, and the freedom which it can bring, can only be sought and appreciated when the cloaks of self-deception are cast off, and true confession made. All the effects of evil: poverty, oppression, abuse, greed, unrestrained ambition, jealousy and envy, need to be named and their causes acknowledged. But in Church and society this must be done not in a manner which accuses others from a position of false innocence, but in a way which recognises mutual culpability and the shared need for forgiveness. In this world we are all sinners and all stand before the one Lord, the one true, pure victim, who alone brings us forgiveness.

At a personal level, too, we must learn to name and acknowledge the victims of our sins. We come closer to forgiveness when we name those whom we have hurt, holding them in our consciousness and in our prayer. We need to attend to them, too, listening to the painful account of their suffering, sensing with them the true effect of our waywardness, accepting it for what it is: the fruit of sin. In recent years the Church as a body has had to face the pain caused by some of its members, not least by a small number of its priests and religious, in their acts of child abuse and sexual sinfulness. This is a long and painful process and one which sears deeply into the hearts of all. Yet this naming of the victim, and the willingness to feel unambiguously the effect of sin, is an essential part of the pattern of salvation spelt out in the suffering of Christ.

The icon of the crucified Christ as the source of forgiveness is focused even more clearly in the image of the Lamb. He is the Lamb of God who takes away the sins of the world. This familiar expression of faith, proclaimed during every Mass, sums up the deepest meaning of forgiveness.

The lamb is, of course, a traditional image of innocence. The freshness of spring is captured in the newly-born lamb, struggling to stand and making those first, carefree, jumps into the air. The lamb is helpless. When the time comes he is led to the slaughter. Resistance is useless. The lamb represents well the innocent victim, the one in whom no guilt or guile is to be found.

The lamb is also an ancient symbol of sacrifice. In the history of the people of Israel, the shedding of the blood of a lamb is the action which brings them to safety in their defining moment of exodus from Egypt. They mark their houses with its blood as a mark of their election by God as the Chosen People:

That night I will go through the land of Egypt and strike down all the first-born in the land of Egypt, man and beast alike, and I shall deal out punishment to all the gods of Egypt, I am Yahweh! The blood shall serve to mark the houses that you live in. When I see the blood I will pass over you and you shall escape the destroying plague when I strike the land of Egypt. This day is to be a day of remembrance for you, and you must celebrate it as a feast in Yahweh's honour (Exod 12:12-14).

Salvation in the blood of the lamb, the covenant between God and Moses sealed in the blood of a lamb, and indeed the blood of the Temple sacrifices (cf Lev 16:1 ff), are, of course, clear prefigurings of the saving death of Jesus. His work of reconciliation, his gift of forgiveness, is summed up in this image of the blood of the lamb. Here we touch the heart of the mystery. Here all its elements come together. Before this image, and this reality, we must stand in awe.

Forgiveness and Wounds

The work of forgiveness is fulfilled in the shedding of the blood of the innocent one, the Lamb of God. Not only is he the saving victim, but the salvation he brings comes precisely from the shedding of his blood, lost through the wounds made in his body. Now we can identify even more precisely the source of that longed-for forgiveness: the wounds and the blood of Christ.

This is a truth which was grasped more fully in times before ours. The history of medieval art, for example, testifies so eloquently to the veneration in which the wounds of Christ were held. In Britain, churches were filled with the image of the wounded Christ. Often the wounded body of Christ, supported by angels, was portrayed above the altar itself, sometimes hidden by curtains until the moment of consecration in the Mass. This was eloquent testimony to a deep and popular appreciation of the forgiveness brought by Christ through the shedding of his blood. That blood was most precious. Even one drop was known to be sufficient for the forgiveness of sins. Hence angels were depicted catching in chalices the precious blood of Christ as he hung on the cross. Here a profound theology, and psychology, was being taught in a way that all could understand.[1]

---

[1] *The Stripping of the Altars*, Eamon Duffy, Yale University Press, 1992; *The History of British Art*, Andrew Graham Dixon, BBC Publications, 1996

In some places the imagery was even more explicit. The Church itself, the community of forgiveness and reconciliation, was depicted being born in the flow of blood and water from the side of Christ. Here a great act of birth is taking place. The entire life of grace, the life of the Holy Spirit in us, comes to birth in that blood and water.

> Do you wish to learn from another source the power of this blood? See where it begins to flow, from what spring it flowed down from the cross, from the Master's side. The Gospel relates that when Christ had died and was still hanging on the cross, the soldier approached him and pierced his side with the spear, and at once there came out water and blood. The one was a symbol of baptism, the other of the mysteries. The soldier then, pierced his side; he breached the wall of the holy temple, and I found the treasure and acquired the wealth... It was from his side, then, that Christ formed the Church, as from the side of Adam he formed Eve (St John Chrysostom, *Instruction to Catechumens*, 3:13-19).

These powerful images of blood that is shed are disturbing to us today. We tend to shy away from such matters. In fact this sense of not being at ease in the presence of any flow of blood has been brought to the fore again in the knowledge that diseases such as AIDS are transmitted in the transfer of even small amounts of blood. Today we protect ourselves against blood. So, too, the strong images of childbirth, with its flows of blood and 'water' are not normally in our religious vocabulary. Yet they speak strongly, especially to those who have experienced that reality. These powerful images, the flow of blood, the reality of new birth, can open up for us something of the power of the blood of Christ. We need to recover a sense of that power if our appreciation of these central mysteries of our faith is to be as profound and fruitful as it should be.

The wounds and the blood of Christ are, then, the source of all forgiveness. The power of God works through the most evident weakness and helplessness of Christ. The same is true for us, too. St Paul reminds us often that our weaknesses are God's strength (2 Cor 4), our foolishness God's wisdom (1 Cor 1). This truth can give us a new way of approaching our own weaknesses, our own wounds. They, too, when brought to Christ, can become the source of healing and forgiveness. For the work of the Spirit God requires not so much our strengths as our wounds. Through them the power of the Spirit can flow in us. Today, both personally and as a Church, we need to heed this invitation. When we can learn to face and name the woundedness of our nature then we can be healed. Paradoxically, wherever the Body of Christ, our human family, is wounded and bleeding, there is to be found the moment of healing grace.

The Precious Blood

The event of our salvation through the blood of Christ is made present to us now in the sacrifice of the Mass. In this context, therefore, we must come to a fresh appreciation of the presence and power of this blood. The blood of Christ is the source of our dignity and worth (1 Cor 6:20). The Mass is a hymn of praise for the gift of God's life in us 'his free gift to us, in the Beloved, in whom, through his blood, we gain our freedom, the forgiveness of our sins' (Eph 1:17). It makes present to us, again and again, that action of total self-giving of the Son to the Father, a giving that cost his very self. The shedding of his blood is, therefore, an act and a revelation of his love. His life's blood is the token of his life's love: to do the will of the Father. And the will of the Father is that not one should be lost, not one overpowered by the grip of evil with its endless downward spiral of anger, oppression, deceit and revenge. To raise again to the Father the blood of Christ is, therefore, to be drawn into that saving self-sacrifice which alone overcomes all evil. To gaze on the chalice at the moment of consecration is to gaze on the source of our protection against all evil. To receive the blood of the Lord in communion is to be bathed again in its stream of love and forgiveness.

The widespread return to the practice of most people being able to receive the precious blood of the Lord in Holy Communion is most welcome. Yet it is a practice and a moment which I fear is still not properly understood. To receive the blood of the Lord is an act of such awesome significance that we ought to be overwhelmed by the moment. Yet it is so often a casual afterthought following the more familiar reception of the sacred host, the body of the Lord. Of course it is true that both the sacred species contain the whole presence of Christ, body and blood. But the power of the symbolism of each can be more fully appreciated if both are part of the action of communion. A more thorough catechesis is surely now required concerning the deeper meaning of this sharing of the blood of the Lord.

'Behold the Lamb of God, behold him who takes away the sins of the world.' Every time we hear these amazing words the whole mystery of salvation is being announced and effected. Through the wounds of Christ, the willing and innocent Lamb, the blood of our forgiveness is poured out. In it we are washed clean. It is the blood of rebirth. In it we are reborn. When we know we are faced with evil, we can seek shelter in the shadow of this chalice. When we have sinned, we can come to drink more deeply at that source of life and wholeness.

The blood of the Lamb is also the promise of the wholeness that still lies ahead. It is the foretaste of the new wine of heaven, the wine of the final marriage feast of the Lamb (Rev 19:9). The robes of the saints have been washed white in this blood, as we see in those marvellous images in the Book of Revelation:

> After that I saw a huge number, impossible to count, of people from every nation, race, tribe and language; they were standing in front of the throne and in front of the Lamb, dressed in white robes and holding palms in their hands... One of the elders then spoke, and asked me, 'Do you know who these people are, dressed in white robes, and where they have come from?' I answered him, 'You can tell me, my lord'. Then he said, 'These are the people who have been through the great persecution, and because they have washed their robes white again in the blood of the Lamb, they now stand in front of God's throne and serve him day and night in his sanctuary; and the One who sits on the throne will spread his tent over them. They will never hunger or thirst again; neither the sun nor scorching wind will ever plague them, because the Lamb who is at the throne will be their shepherd and will lead them to springs of living water; and God will wipe away all tears from their eyes' (Rev 7:-17).

Until that time comes we bring ourselves to the sacrament of that precious blood to be marked by it, cleansed by it, claimed by it. The blood of Christ, the wounds of Christ, disclose to us the true nature of forgiveness. Recovering this truth, and all it unfolds about our own vulnerability and the sources of forgiveness, will, I believe, do more than anything to bring about a renewal of the gift of repentance, forgiveness and reconciliation which we so urgently need today.

> Blood of my Saviour, bathe me in thy tide
> Wash me in waters flowing from thy side.
> Strength and protection, may thy passion be,
> O blessed Jesus hear and answer me.
> Deep in thy wounds, Lord, hide and shelter me
> So shall I never, never part from thee
> (*Anima Christi*, Soul of my Saviour).

Questions for Reflection

1. The phrase 'the sins of the world' is powerful and evocative. What comes to your mind when you hear and reflect on it?

2. Have you ever struggled to forgive another person? What made it so difficult? In what ways did you feel a victim? Could you, perhaps, talk about these things in a group, but without betraying any personal confidences?

3. Have you ever struggled with the strong desire to take revenge, or to 'get even'? What might hold you back?

4. Does the image of the Church being born from the side of Christ, with the flow of blood and water, appeal to you? How does it help you to understand the ways in which God's gifts are given?

5. In your opinion, what more could be done to help people to understand the presence of Christ in the precious blood? Is there any devotion to the precious blood of Christ in your parish, or in your own life?"

6.   Did you know that the red flag was the medieval
     flag of the people because it was the symbol of
     the blood of Christ, shed for all? Everyone could
     wave that flag and shelter under it. With what do
     you associate the red flag?

Prayer

Lord our God, we thank you for the blood of your
Son, the Lamb of God. As we gaze upon that blood
in the chalice raised at Mass, and as we receive it in
Holy Communion, give us your protection against
all evil, both from within and from without. Wash
us clean in this precious blood that we may stand in
the company of your people and come to worship
before your throne of glory. We make this prayer
through Jesus Christ our Lord. Amen.

EIGHT
ITE, MISSA EST

Go in peace, glorifying the Lord by your life

As a child I used to take much pride in following the text of the Mass with great care in my own missal. I found a sense of achievement in knowing precisely which part of the Latin text the priest was saying. I followed more closely than I understood. But one phrase used to puzzle me more than most. I knew only too well that my missal told me the '*Ite, missa est*' meant 'Go forth, the Mass is ended'. But I found the reply, 'Thanks be to God', rather too close for comfort to my own feelings. Were we really supposed to be quite so glad that, at last, the Mass was over? True enough, the rest of Sunday now beckoned, but there seemed to be a lack of reverence in such a response!

The source of my problem lay, of course, in the translation. The word m*issa* is full of meanings quite lost in this translation. It is the root of our word 'mission', and of the word 'Mass' itself. It speaks of a sending forth rather than an ending. It is the giving of a commission, a task, for which we have just been prepared and strengthened. The task is none other than the mission of Christ, received from the Father and now shared with each of us.

Every sacrament contains such an imperative. In celebrating them we receive not only the consolation of their grace, but also the command 'Go and do likewise' (cf John 13:15). In the sacrament of Reconciliation, for example, the imperative is clear: forgive others and do not sin again (cf John 8:11). In the sacrament of marriage the task is that of being a source of love for others, and a sign of God's abiding fidelity. The prayers of blessing over the newly married couple make this clear:

> May God the eternal Father keep you in love with each other, so that the peace of Christ may stay with you and be always in your home. May you always bear witness to the love of God in this world so that the afflicted and the needy will find in you generous friends and welcome you into the joys of heaven (*Roman Missal*, Wedding Mass (A)).

The anointing of the sick, too, contains within it the invitation to unite our sufferings with those of Christ and to make of them an offering. In this perhaps, we see most clearly how the grace of the sacrament actually enables us to do something which left to ourselves we could never achieve. The life of God in us, initiated and strengthened by our celebration of the sacraments, is the source of such a new way of living. The requirements of that new life are written into the text of the sacraments themselves.

Another way of putting this is to say that every sacrament contains within it both an inner moment and an outward movement. In each sacrament we are drawn first of all into deeper intimacy with God. In each God shares the divine life with us. Such moments require real interiority, silence and recollection. Yet each sacrament also contains its own outward movement, a reaching out to others in new patterns of love: with welcome, with forgiveness, with compassion, with a renewed sense of being brothers and sisters in the Lord. This dual movement is no more than a reflection of the life and love of God. The inner mystery of the Trinitarian love of the Father, Son and Holy Spirit also flows outward in the constant act of creation.

The rich reflection of the Second Vatican Council on the nature of the Church, found in the Dogmatic Constitution *Lumen Gentium*, is, in its own way, a meditation on the 'inner moment' of the Church's being. It is completed by the Pastoral Constitution *Gaudium et Spes*, commonly known as The Church in the Modern World. In turn this is a reflection on the 'outward movement' of the Church, its place and mission in the wider society.

A Missionary Church

Since Vatican II, various Synods of Bishops have reflected on different aspects of the mystery of the Church. The Synod of 1974 had as its theme the missionary task of the Church. Its final reflection, issued by the Holy Father, boldly asserted that the Church:

> exists in order to evangelise, that is to say in order to preach and teach, to be the channel of the gift of grace, to reconcile sinners with God, and to perpetuate Christ's sacrifice in the Mass, which is the memorial of his death and glorious Resurrection (*Evangelii Nuntiandi*, para 14).

In other words all the gifts given to the Church have, as their sole purpose, the announcing of the Gospel in word and deed, in every corner and aspect of human living. The Church exists for this purpose, which in itself gives glory and praise to God.

A further Synod of Bishops, in 1987, reflected on the role and vocation of the baptised in the life and mission of the Church. The final reflection of that Synod, the document *Christifideles Laici*, opened with a meditation on the parable of the workers in the vineyard (Matt 20:1-16). As the image was developed, it became clear that the vineyard in which the baptised faithful are called to work is not the inner life of the Church but the secular world. In other words, the proper task of the vast majority of the baptised is to live the Gospel in the circumstances of everyday life: the home, the workplace, the places of fun and relaxation, the streets and the markets. The mission proclaimed at the end of every Mass is this: 'Go from here now, to love, glorify and serve the Lord in all that you do during this day, this week, in every circumstance, in every place, without exception.'

Often our first instinct is quite the opposite. We may have found such consolation and peace in the celebration of Mass that we want to remain in its embrace, in its 'inner moment'. This, of course, was the temptation faced by St Peter at the Transfiguration. 'Lord', he said, 'it is wonderful for us to be here.' He wanted to stay, to make the moment permanent. But the Lord's instructions were clear: they had to come down from that mountain, turn towards the city and face the crowds. They had to be ready even for suffering and the reality of the cross (cf Matt 17:1 ff).

Obviously much work is needed, within the community of the Church, in order for it to be strong and sufficiently nourished in teaching and prayer to carry out this primary task of being a distinctive leaven in the world. God gives all the gifts needed for this nurturing to be effectively carried out. The Church must always be on the alert to recognise and utilise these gifts. Those who have received the sacrament of Holy Orders are, in a particular way, charged with this task. It is they who have received the imperative of making sure that the life of the Church is deeply rooted in the 'order' which comes from God in Christ. The particular task of the bishop and priest is to draw together the talents given in the Church and to ensure that they are used for the building up of the Body for its mission in the world. But in having this task, those in Holy Orders are exceptions; they are the odd ones out. They do not reflect the normal pattern of Christian living.

Perhaps this is well illustrated by the simple discipline that the ordained members of the Church must withdraw from the party political life of a country. They must do so as a sign that the Church draws its mandate and its message from Christ and not from any other source. At that level the Church must stand at a critical distance from party politics. But for the majority of the Church, the faithful laity, involvement in the detail of political life is a particularly important part of the mission of the Church. The Gospel of Christ impinges on every effort to construct a more just and peaceful society. It is the mission of those sent out at the end of Mass to roll up their sleeves and get involved, as members of the Church, in matters just such as these.

A Mighty Force for Good

The proclamation *Ite, missa est* ought to release into our society a mighty force for all that is truly good, truly of God. But does it do so? The first impression must be that it does not. Otherwise why is its impact not much more evident? Yet perhaps we come to that conclusion too quickly. Who can imagine what the history of our human family would have been like without the revelation of God in Christ and its courageous proclamation over the centuries by countless 'missionaries'? Without the Judeo-Christian tradition would the dignity of every person have been understood and developed as it is today? Would there have been such deep care and respect for life, especially at its most vulnerable moments? Would the enterprise of human knowledge, research and learning have survived the darker ages without the commitment of the followers of Christ? This is not, of course, to claim that Christians alone have held to these insights. Nor is it to deny that in every age the living of the Gospel has been characterised by profound ambiguities, some of which have left as many problems as benefits. But it is to indicate, however briefly, that the Gospel is a potent force in our story. It has been and it can be so today.

Perhaps, with a little more reflection, the words with which we end the Mass could resonate again with some of the excitement of the mission which they indicate. The mission we are given is one of bringing the best out of every situation, bringing a vision of how life is meant to be, an idealism which is not a remote dream but a promise of God. The mission we receive is one which requires our most fertile imagination and our most resolute efforts. It is as broad as the whole panorama of life and as intimate as our most treasured relationships. It is an adventure without equal. Let us look at some of its dimension.

The Environment

This mission is a call to service to the whole of the created order. Over and over again, young people approaching me for confirmation choose the name of Francis. The saint of Assisi speaks to them of their passionate concern for the well-being of creation. The Gospel of Christ not only spells out a vision of the unity and true purpose of the created order, but it also presents us with some principles on which to understand our part in creation. Environmental issues must find their place in our missionary concerns. They have already found a place in the hearts of the young. The rest of us must catch up!

So many aspects of this challenge lie before us. May I stress just one. No concern for the environment can ignore questions of the levels of consumption of the world's resources which we, in the developed world, both demand and take for granted. The call to poverty and simplicity which lies at the heart of the Gospel has many dimensions to it. Among them, most certainly, is an appreciation of the fact that we are to be stewards of creation and not simply consumers. The tradition which flows from Assisi is indeed strong and illuminating in this regard.

Quiet Witnesses

The mission we announce at the end of Mass is also one of service to the human community. As the famous opening words of *Gaudium et Spes* state, nothing which is truly human fails to find an echo in the hearts and minds of the followers of Christ (para 1). The concerns and trials of our local community must be those of its Christian members in a rather special way. This applies to every aspect of life, not just to the more obvious, public or political ones.

I remember being moved profoundly when listening to a sculptor explaining how his faith and work in the local community were intertwined. He ran evening classes in painting and sculpture. In them he and his pupils were trying to explore and express the depth of human experience. He knew he searched by the light of Christ. Yet he found it impossible to say so explicitly, such was the resistance of those with whom he worked to many aspects of the Christian message as they had experienced it. Yet express his faith he must. He told us that he did so by writing a private poem. It was entitled *Why I cannot name You*. It read as a kind of apology to the Lord himself. Yet his fidelity to the Lord was beyond question. And so too was his missionary endeavour. He joined wholeheartedly with his contemporaries in their search for truth and light, and in their attempts to express that truth in their art. He did not impose himself or his faith. He served the quest, humbly keeping the Word of life to himself until he thought it would be received. Towards the end of one long journey of discovery, a fellow artist looked more closely at a study he was completing. He said that he thought he could see a hidden light shining out of it. The moment had then arrived, and the Name could be spoken. At that moment a journey of faith for his fellow artist began.

To bear witness to the truth of the Gospel in our contemporary urban society is not easy. Yet over and over again I find wonderful examples of people doing so. While in a parish I often ask to see the sick and the housebound. Visiting them I see so many examples of people living out the imperative of the sacrament of marriage. Neighbours offer unceasing care for the sick and housebound. They do so almost as a matter of course. They reach out to those in risk of isolation, making available to them some of the strength and resilience they have found within their own family life. In this they resist the temptation which assails everyone living in cities: that of isolating ourselves from others, of putting up walls of indifference as protection against the heaving crowds and pressing problems.

A Renewed Society

In many ways simple examples such as these illustrate an essential aspect of the mission we all receive: that of exploring ceaselessly the relationship between the individual and the wider community. We need, as a society, a renewed vision of the 'person-in-community' if we are to find proper ways of responding to so many difficulties. Excessive emphases on either the individual or the community have characterised efforts to fashion society. Yet there remains in most people an instinct which recognises our mutual interdependence, at least in a limited way. The Gospel message of radical interdependence and of radical individuality can build on this instinct. If it is to do so, we who receive and try to live that message must engage more energetically in the search. Understandably this teaching has been called 'the Church's best kept secret' and we need to spread this teaching, with its relevance to modern society, much more systematically.'[1]

Yet service such as this is not just the means we use in order to fulfil our mission in Christ. It is also part of the witness which we are to give. The kingdom which we are called to proclaim is signalled as much in the way we do things as in our aims for society. The witness of the way of life of the early Christians first marked them out and drew the attention of others. For

---

[1] *The Common Good*, Bishops' Conference of England and Wales, October 1996

me, this underlines the importance of two particular aspects of contemporary Church life: the efforts being made to develop patterns of collaborative ministry, and the search for visible unity among Christians. Both of these are important aspects of the witness we are to give.

Collaborative ministry, or rather, clear patterns of collaboration and cooperation between the various ministries given to the Church, is an essential aspect of the true face of the Church. The emergence of renewed roles for women and young people in the life and work of the Church are central to this, too. The image which the Church presents, is the image in which most people will see the face of Christ. For this reason it must be as complete and inclusive as possible, one in which gifts are acknowledged and employed for the benefit of all.

Seeking Unity

So, too, the long, slow, search for deeper understanding between Christians is part of the imperative expressed in every celebration of the Mass. As the sacrament of our unity in Christ, it is impossible to come away from the Mass without a renewed sense of the urgency of ecumenism. Not only should we feel more keenly the pain of the divided Body of Christ, but we should also have a developed appreciation of the harm done to our Christian mission by that divided state. The patient striving for new patterns of partnership and joint action between Christians, whether locally or nationally, is part of the imperative of our mission. It is not an optional extra, or, in some strange way, a weakening of our Catholic identity. On the contrary it is so much part of our identity that those who scorn or minimise its importance do real harm to the mission to which they are called.

As a true expression of the life of the Church of Christ, this ecumenism is itself part of the witness that the Church wishes to offer to the world. Ecclesial ecumenism is a sign, a signal, of that wider human ecumenism for which so many strive. The vision of the unity of the human family is so easily wrecked. The powerfully negative aspects of nationalism are but one source of this destructiveness, as has been brutally displayed in the countries of the former Yugoslavia. The work of rebuilding those communities on foundations of ceased hostilities moving towards stability and peace is a long and painful road. It is the work of the Gospel, as many in the armed forces know. So too is the delicate work of achieving the right kind of unity across the countries of Europe. At each level, whether in the Church or in society, the vision of the 'wholeness of all in Christ' is an essential guide and challenge. We proclaim him as the sole redeemer. Without him we will not achieve any of these worthy ambitions.

Ready for Action

As we reflect in this way on our mission in Christ, there are two biblical images which speak powerfully of the task we undertake and the attitude we require. The first is the well- known account of the Annunciation.

On hearing the angel's message, Mary is described as 'deeply disturbed'. She asked herself 'what this greeting could mean'. When the angel explained the purpose of the message, the birth of a son to be called Jesus, Mary replied, 'But how can this come about since I am a virgin?' Then the angel proclaimed the power of God and the action of the Holy Spirit, speaking not only of Mary herself but also of her kinswoman, Elizabeth. Then Mary responds. In doing so she sets the paradigm for all disciples. She says, 'I am the handmaid of the Lord, let what you have said be done to me' (Luke 1:26-38).

As a first step, we must note that Mary did not simply indicate her agreement to the plan once it had been explained. Her response was not, 'All right, in that case I will do it.' Rather she goes further. She opens herself totally to the will of God, professing complete readiness to do not only what has been explained to her, but anything that may be required:

'Let it be done to me.' In this active readiness Mary teaches us the very heart of discipleship, the attitude that should be ours as we leave Mass, commissioned for our task in the world. We come to the end of Mass not only having completed an exercise, not only having participated in a saving action, not only with strength for future labour. Rather, we come to the end of Mass with a new awareness, a renewed awareness, of the constant, saving presence of God. We go from the celebration of Mass with a new heart, attentive to the promptings of God wherever we may sense them. In the words of the Psalmist:

Like the eyes of a servant
on the hands of her mistress
So our eyes are on the Lord our God
Until he show us his mercy (Ps 122).

The prompting of God, God's messages, God's angels, may come in all sorts of circumstances: in the needs of a neighbour, in the demands of a child, in the intricacies of an academic debate, in the midst of political manoeuvres. The person who has a heart raised to new levels of attentiveness through the celebration of the saving mysteries will try to sense these invitations and respond to them with courage. At this level of awareness we grasp again that all initiative in fact comes from the Lord. Our celebration of Mass teaches us this 'readiness of heart' and builds up in us a determination to let nothing again obscure or hinder this truth.

St Clare, who is such a reliable guide in so many ways, writes of this alertness and this determination:

> What you hold, may you always hold.
> What you do, may you always do
> and never abandon.
> But with swift pace, light step,
> and unswerving feet,
> so that even your steps stir up no dust,
> go forward
> securely, joyfully, and swiftly,
> on the path of prudent happiness
> believing nothing,
> agreeing with nothing
> which would dissuade you from this resolution
> or which would place a stumbling block
> for you on the way
> so that you may offer your vows to the Most High
> in the pursuit of that perfection
> to which the Spirit of the Lord has called you
> (St Clare, *Second Letter to Blessed Agnes of Prague*).

Practical Wisdom

The second scriptural image to guide our fulfilment of this mission is to be found in Chapter 3 of the First Book of Kings. Here Solomon is invited by the Lord, in a dream, to ask for any gift. In reply Solomon reflects on his inadequacy for the office of king, inherited from his father David:

I am a very young man, unskilled in leadership. Your servant finds himself in the midst of this people of yours that you have chosen, a people so many its number cannot be counted or reckoned. Give your servant a heart to understand how to discern between good and evil, for who could govern this people of yours that is so great?

God is pleased that Solomon has shown such perceptiveness in this request for wisdom, rather than asking for riches or victories over his enemies. So God grants his request and bestows upon Solomon long life and riches too. Next we read:

Then Solomon returned to Jerusalem and stood before the ark of the covenant of Yahweh; he offered holocausts and communion sacrifices, and held a banquet for all his servants (1 Kings 3:4-15).

It seems to me that hidden in this prayer, in this episode, is all that is required for fruitful discipleship and mission. We are in need of discernment. We need to know the priorities to which we should attend and to know the steps by which best to pursue them. Every practical circumstance requires such wisdom. It is indeed right that we constantly ask for such a gift. But even more remarkable is the insistence of the last line. The fruit of such wisdom is a party for the servants! Words and actions which encourage one another are so important. The daily effort of so many is easily overlooked, especially when a new project comes onto the parish agenda. The most important work of discipleship is nearly always hidden. It does not draw attention to itself, nor does it seek a mention in the parish newsletter. But wisdom instructs us not to forget words of mutual encouragement for the least of those at work in the kingdom of God, the least of the labourers in the vineyard of the Lord.

> The eyes of faith behold a wonderful scene: that of a countless number of lay people, both women and men, busy at work in their daily life and activity, often times far from view and quite unacclaimed by the world, unknown to the world's great personages but nonetheless looked upon in love by the Father, untiring labourers who work in the Lord's vineyard. Confident and steadfast through the power of God's grace, these are the humble yet great builders of the Kingdom of God in history (*Christifideles Laici*, para 17).

This is the task to which we are sent at the end of Mass. We have explored our dependence on God and entered more deeply into the mystery of God's action in our world. We have been nourished by the Word of God and the Body and Blood of the Lord. Now we set out again on our pilgrimage of faith, with the wonderful promise of future glory ringing in our ears. Every one of these faithful disciples will be celebrated by the Lord and lavished with unexpected love.

Questions for Reflection

1. Do you appreciate some further moments of quiet prayer at the end of Mass? Are such moments possible? Would you rather leave the church immediately and get on with the work of the day?

2. At the end of Mass you hear the words 'Go in peace to love and serve the Lord.' On most days, what does this mean to you? When, in the course of the day, do you get the sense of 'serving the Lord'.

3. Which occupations or professions seem to present the greatest difficulties for those who want to let the gospel shape their daily living? What support or encouragement do such professionals need?

4. Which issues of today's popular agenda – such as peace, the environment, racial justice, etc – seem to be most lacking in the way in which you, or the parish, pray? What could you do about this?

5. Could you be doing a bit more to get to know and understand Catholic social teaching?

6. Could you use the gospel narrative of the Annunciation as a starting point for imaginative prayer? Can you imagine being present with Mary when the angel comes? What do you feel? What thoughts pass through your mind? What does the angel's message say to you? Perhaps you could share some of your experience in prayer with others.

Prayer

Lord our God, you continue your saving work in our world in countless, unseen ways. We thank you for the hidden gifts you give. We ask you to instil in our hearts a readiness to serve you in our families, our neighbourhood, and in our working lives. Help us to rejoice with those who share our vision for your world so that together we may bring the light of your love into our common life. We make this prayer through Christ our Lord. Amen.

NINE

THE PROMISE
OF FUTURE GLORY

*May the Body of Christ keep me safe
for eternal life. May the Blood of Christ
keep me safe for eternal life.*

A s a newly ordained priest I served for a few years in St Mary's Church in Wigan. Around the walls of its sanctuary are carved the words of St Thomas Aquinas in which he expresses most succinctly the Church's faith in the Mass. I used to read and reflect on those words quite often. They seemed so well placed:

*O sacrum convivium, in quo Christus sumitur,
Recolitur memoria passionis eius*

*Mens impletur gratia
Et futurae gloriae nobis pignus datur*

O sacred banquet, in which Christ is received,
the memory of his passion renewed,
the mind is filled with grace
and a pledge of future glory is given to us.

The Mass is indeed a convivium, a sharing of life, a true communion. In it Christ gives himself to us in such a way that we are 'taken into' him. The Passion of Christ becomes a living memory, its effectiveness made present to us, filling our minds with grace, and giving us a promise of future glory. Perhaps the weight of the word *pignus* is worth considering. It can be translated not only as a 'promise' but also as a 'pledge'. I once heard it explained as the 'down-payment' which secures the new purchase, even if the whole exchange is not yet complete. In the death and resurrection of Christ our future glory is secure. For our part we must cling to him. Just before receiving Holy Communion the priest says quietly: 'May the Body of Christ keep me safe for eternal life. May the Blood of Christ keep me safe for eternal life'. These words used to be said as each person received Holy Communion, but are now replaced with the shorter phrase: 'The Body of Christ.' The act of faith is the same: through this communion with Christ may I be brought to the future glory of eternal life.

But what is this future glory for which we pray? What can we know about the promise which lies ahead, about the kingdom we are to inherit? How does its hope give shape to our efforts each day?

Hints of Heaven

There are a number of places to which we can turn in order to catch glimpses of this future. All are tenuous, for we simply do not know. But the hints are there.

Some people concentrate on the so-called 'near death' experiences which are so carefully recorded and studied. One friend of mine told me that as her mother was approaching death, with clarity and calmness, she asked her if she had any clearer intuition of the life which was to come. 'Oh, yes!' replied her mother with pleasure in her voice. 'Tell me about it', said the daughter eagerly. But at that moment her mother lapsed back into deep sleep!

It seems to me that, if we are made in the image and likeness of God, hints of this future glory must be written into our very nature. We have strong instincts about heaven, for there is a restlessness in us which will only be satisfied when we come to our final home.

One seems particularly clear: heaven is surely a freedom from sickness and pain and from all the limitations and frustrations of our present condition. Sometimes the intensity of this longing for release is hard to bear or to observe, especially in those we love. We come to share their longing 'that it might be over soon'. Moments such as these test faith, sometimes to the limit: is this suffering and approaching death a passage to final fulfilment, or is it the last agony before oblivion? With good reason, then, many speak of these final times in a person's life as the most important journey of all. To keep company with the sick and the dying is to serve the Lord in a most delicate and fruitful way. It is, indeed, to stand on the threshold of heaven.

There are other longings and frustrations which give us a glimpse of the future glory to which we are invited. I think society is full of them. For example, freedom to speak as we wish is written so deeply into our hearts that many give their lives for that right. This freedom is basic to the human person, as an intelligent, reflecting being. Not to be able to speak one's mind is indeed a denial of a very fundamental right. It carries corresponding duties with it, of course! I will always remember a week I spent in San Salvador at the time of the civil war. 'Be wary of what you say in any public place,' I was told. 'Be especially careful in taxis! You never know who is listening.' For me this was quite a shock. Yet for so many people round the world it is their daily experience. The restoration of freedom of speech is always met with an explosion of relief, as a people can once again express themselves, their anxieties, their opinions, without undue restraint.

Perhaps it is not too surprising that heaven is often described in terms of ceaseless praise! The Book of Revelation, for example, tells us that in heaven:

Day and night they never stopped singing:
'Holy, Holy, Holy
is the Lord God, the Almighty;
he was, he is and he is to come' (Rev 4:8).

Then I heard all the living things in creation – everything that lives in the air, and on the ground, and under the ground, and in the sea, crying;
To the One seated on the throne be all praise,
honour, glory and power, for ever and ever'
(Rev 5:13).

Freedom of speech is, then, the order of the day! In heaven it finds its final purpose: the praise of God.

In like manner there is also an instinct in us to want to take part in the activity going on around us, especially if it affects us directly. The desire to participate is, I think, another signpost to heaven. Who can ever forget the moving pictures of long and winding queues of people waiting patiently for hours or days, in the hot sun, to vote in the first full elections in South Africa or the risks taken by people in Iraq, in this first free election? The desire to participate is deep indeed. It is closely linked to the desire to speak freely, to let one's views be known. It is to claim a right to be part of the activity of bringing order and pattern to a way of life, whether it be in 'communion of life' celebrated in the Eucharist, on which we have been reflecting, includes within it affirmation that this desire to participate will indeed come to a fulfilment when that sacramental promise is fulfilled.

The desire to participate is a measure of our dignity and worth. It is complemented by that aspect of our faith which reminds us that God is present in every person, no matter how insignificant he or she may seem, and may indeed be speaking through that person. Democratic patterns may not be the most efficient ways of 'getting things done'; but they do seem to correspond more fittingly to a true understanding of the dignity of the human person. In recent decades, the Church has come to express this view in a quite formal manner.

> The Church values the democratic system inasmuch as it ensures the participation of citizens in making political choices, guarantees to the governed the possibility both of electing and holding accountable those who govern them, and of replacing them through peaceful means when appropriate... Authentic democracy is possible only in a state ruled by law and on the basis of a correct conception of the human person….. It must be observed in this regard that if there is no ultimate truth

to guide and direct political activity, then ideas and convictions can easily be manipulated for reasons of power. As history demonstrates, a democracy a state, a school, religious order, parish or family. The without values easily turns into open or thinly disguised totalitarianism (John Paul II, *Centesimus Annus*, para 46).

The dignity of the human person is not only underpinned by eternal values and ultimate truth, but it will find its eventual fulfilment in the wholeness of heaven.

More Hints of Heaven

In a similar fashion it is surely possible to see hints of heaven in other aspects of the longings which characterise the human spirit at its best. The battle against crippling poverty, against blatant oppression, attempts to rectify miscarriages of justice, all testify to the strength of instinct that cries out 'such things should not be'. Heaven must be that time and place where they no longer exist. That is the promise we have received.

The Preface of the Mass for the Feast of Christ the King puts well this instinct for heaven:

...as eternal priest and King of all creation... he might present to the immensity of your

majesty, an eternal and universal kingdom,
a kingdom of truth and life,
a kingdom of holiness and grace,
a kingdom of justice, love and peace
(*Roman Missal*).

The prayer for the coming of a 'kingdom of truth' addresses a profound longing in every person. We long to know the truth of a situation. We have that 'unrestricted desire' to know and to make sense – find the truth – of all around us. The Book of Genesis acknowledges this in describing the basic temptation as that of wanting the knowledge that is proper only to God. In God that longing will be fulfilled. But for now we face the difficulty of discerning truth from falsehood, life-giving knowledge from mere information.

The 'kingdom of truth', for which we long, will bring to an end the ambiguities with which we constantly live. In this life we are never totally sure. Doubt can seep into even our most strongly constructed convictions. And perhaps it should. For our present condition is not to know anything with absolute certainty: the love of another, an account of any historical event, a mathematical or scientific theory, an assessment of our own or another's goodness. For now we must live, in the midst of ambiguity, by probability and trust. This often leads us into situations of conflict and dissidence, where one person or another protests that an account of events, a judgement of another, is totally wrong. Hardly surprisingly we have constructed complicated systems of arbitration by which we try to settle the ambiguities. But still the dissatisfaction lingers. It will be removed only in the kingdom of truth itself.

In similar fashion, this kingdom will herald the end of all conflicts of authority and struggles for power. What a relief that will be! In this kingdom the simplicity of truth will reveal the correct relationship between every living thing and its source and purpose in life. Put more simply, God will be all in all, and all our striving shall cease. For this reason the description of heaven includes the phrase 'a kingdom of peace'. There the integration of all aspects of life will be complete. A harmony of forces will be achieved, within ourselves, between us, and within the natural world. This is surely what St Paul is hinting at in his words in the Letter to the Church in Rome:

> I think that what we suffer in this life can never be compared to the glory, as yet unrevealed, which is waiting for us. The whole creation is eagerly waiting for God to reveal his sons. It was not for any fault on the part of creation that it was made unable to attain its purpose, it was made so by God; but creation still retains the hope of being freed, like us, from its slavery to decadence, to enjoy the same freedom

and glory as the children of God. From the beginning till now the entire creation, as we know, has been groaning in one great act of giving birth; and not only creation, but all of us who possess the first-fruits of the Spirit, we too groan inwardly as we wait for our bodies to be set free (Rom 8:18-23).

The task of integrating our sexuality is, perhaps, one of the aspects of our present condition which causes us to groan more than most. This might be particularly true for those who strive to live celibate chastity, but I suspect it is so for many more. After all, the chastity within marriage that Christian living requires is not easily achieved either. One of the most helpful insights into this aspect of our pilgrimage comes from St Clare. She manages to cast the quest for true chastity in such positive terms, whereas it is so easily thought of as a negative requirement. For her chastity, or virginity, comes from true and profound love. Such love will only be fully experienced in the 'kingdom of love'. The task then is always before us. It is never too late to start again, to strive to grow in that love which alone can bring us the integration for which we long. St Clare writes:

When you have loved him, you shall be chaste; when you have touched him, you shall become pure; when you have accepted him, you shall be a virgin, him whose power is stronger, whose appearance more beautiful, whose love more tender, whose courtesy more gracious, in whose embrace you are already caught up (St Clare, *First Letter to Blessed Agnes of Prague*).

All is Gift

Throughout this book I have been stressing the priority which we must give to the action of God. That is a key struggle for people of our age. We are so used to achieving things by our own efforts and taking responsibility for everything. These are good and important attitudes, but they are deceptive if we hold them to be the whole story. So too at times we are tempted to believe that we must construct the kingdom out of our own efforts and that, if we cannot be sure of constructing a kingdom that lasts after death, we must construct one here and now. Of course that is a proper desire. But it is not the whole story and to present it as if it were is to mislead.

In fact the more essential part of the truth is that the kingdom we are to inherit is a pure gift. Like all which we have and are, it comes to us from God. We cannot claim it as our own, and to do so risks our very salvation. These words spell out that message:

When Yahweh has brought you into the land which he swore to your fathers Abraham, Isaac and Jacob that he would give you, with great and

203

> prosperous cities not of your building, houses
> full of good things not furnished by you, wells
> you did not dig, vineyards and olives you did not
> plant, when you have eaten these and had your
> fill, then take care you do not forget Yahweh
> who brought you out of the land of Egypt, out
> of the house of slavery (Deut 6:10-12).

The richness of the vision of the Promised Land given at that time to the people of Israel is a sign of the love which the Lord wishes to lavish on those who are truly his people. Cities, houses, wells, vineyards, olives, all the achievements of a civilisation, were given in abundance in order to demonstrate the more fundamental truth: that salvation is not to be found in any of them, but in the work of the Lord. In fact, such abundance of itself can bring its own confusion and imprisonment. I cannot rid my imagination of the image of a young highly successful commodities dealer I heard of once. He owned and lived in a magnificent Swiss chateau. His wealth was more or less unlimited. Yet he was so caught up in the business of making money that in fact he lived in one room, furnished only with a camp-bed and a telephone. Perhaps his salvation lay in this simplicity. Or perhaps it was a sign of an inner emptiness and compulsiveness. I shall never know. But I hope that he, too, could recall the Gospel warning that self-made success is, in the last analysis, an obstacle on our pathway to eternal life.

The Banquet

Yet perhaps the most powerful and abiding picture of heaven that we are given in the Scriptures is that of the banquet. This image captures so much of the extravagance of God's love, so much of its exuberance. The banquet must be filled (Luke 14:23); it is a banquet of finest wines and richest food (Isa 25:6); it is a banquet for which all are provided with the necessary attire (Matt 2:12, Rev 7:9). It is a banquet which is entirely the free gift of grace.

Anyone who has seen the remarkable film Babette's Feast will know how richly this image can be developed. Babette uses all her savings and all her skill as a chef to provide, unexpectedly, the most amazing banquet in the remote village where she lives and works. The film lingers over every detail of the event. It is as sumptuous as it is unexpected. And at the end of the meal the participants, on whom she has waited at table, leave with their sharp differences being reconciled. The Eucharistic themes of the film are not difficult to detect!

The banquet of heaven is, of course, a wedding feast. It celebrates new beginnings, new life, the promise of new birth. It marks the completion of a preparatory period: the time of groaning. Now all is complete and the feast must simply begin. Yet we have to remember, too, that it is the wedding feast of the Lamb. Even here, in his glory, the image in which we must learn to see the Bridegroom is that of the Lamb: the innocent victim, the one who was slain.

The Church is already the Bride. Every Mass celebrates this reality, the sharing of life, the sharing of one body. But the completion of that union is not yet come. Edith Stein expresses these matters so well:

> The Church lives, she is wedded to the Lamb, but the hour of the solemn marriage supper will only arrive when the dragon has been completely conquered and the last of the redeemed have fought their battle to the end.

> Just as the Lamb had to be killed to be raised upon the throne of glory, so the path to glory leads through suffering and the cross for everyone chosen to attend the marriage supper of the Lamb. All who want to be married to the Lamb must allow themselves to be fastened to the cross with him. Everyone marked by the blood of the Lamb is called to this, and that means all the baptised. (Edith Stein, *The Marriage of the Lamb*: For 14 September 1940)[1]

---

[1] From *The Hidden Life: The Collected Works of Edith Stein*, ed. Dr L Gelber and Michael Linsin OCD, trans. W Stein published by the Institute of Carmelite Studies

This, then, is our path to glory. As we go, our task is to do all we can to construct in our world hints of the heaven that lies ahead. We are to set up signposts to heaven, creating oases of heaven here in our midst. In this we cooperate with all who are doing similar work, whether or not that is their understanding. In our care of the sick and the dying; in our passion for the truth; in the clarity of thought in which the true foundations of life are made clear; in our search for harmony in love and friendships; in our attitude to possessions and wealth; in the love we are prepared to lavish, even unexpectedly, on friends and visitors alike; in all these ways we are keeping alive the rumour of heaven, the promise of a true home. We know we are the inheritors of that promise. But we are to proclaim it, in deed and in word, so that others too may share in its joy.

The disciples of the Lord, in their journey, were undoubtedly spurred on by the experience of Peter, James and John on Mount Tabor. The sight of the Lord transfigured in all his glory must have been talked about by them all on many occasions. The glimpse of such glory will have stayed with them, encouraged them and strengthened them throughout their lives. In that moment they saw, with stunning clarity, the glory of the Lord and the majesty of God. Such an experience, which must have sustained them in even the darkest hour, pointed the way to the final fulfilment of their discipleship.

In the Orthodox tradition of Christianity, the Feast of the Transfiguration of the Lord is given much more prominence than it is in the Western tradition. This feast celebrates not only the glory of the Lord, but also the final destiny of the believer. Here, in this feast, the implications of the coming of the Lord in the flesh are spelt out. The Incarnation leads to the Transfiguration and from there to final glory. Not surprisingly then icons of the Transfiguration are to be found decorating Christmas cribs and other portrayals of the birth of Christ. When the Lord comes to share our flesh, then we are being invited to share his glory.

In some measure every celebration of the Mass is a celebration of the Transfiguration. In the action of the Mass the glory of the Lord is revealed and celebrated. He is again raised in glory. He is again proclaimed as the fulfilment of God's law and promise. Our vocation, too, is revealed and celebrated in the Mass, for united with Christ, sealed by his blood and nourished by his body, we come to live not for ourselves but for him. And in him the promise of our future glory is made secure. As St Paul writes to the Corinthians:

> All of us, then, reflect the glory of the Lord with uncovered faces; and that same glory, coming from the Lord who is the Spirit, transforms us into his very likeness, in an ever greater degree of glory (2 Cor 3:18).

Words of one of the Fathers of the Church, St Anastasius of Sinai, written for the Feast of the Transfiguration, can be applied to the celebration of the Mass. They can also serve as our final invitation to enter more deeply into the mystery of faith, day by day, as we gather at the altar:

What is more blessed, what is more sublime, what more exalted than to be with God, to be shaped to his likeness, to dwell in the light? Since each one of us has God within him and is transformed into his divine image, let us cry out in joy: 'It is good for us to be here.' For here is all light, and joy, and happiness, and bliss; here the heart is at rest, in peace, serene; here we behold Christ our God; here he comes to dwell with the Father, and as he enters he says: 'Today salvation has been brought to this house'; here with Christ are the countless treasures of eternal blessings; here are the beginnings of the age to come. (St Anastasius of Sinai, Liturgy of the Hours, Feast of the Transfiguration)

Questions for Reflection

1. Have you ever experienced any 'hints of heaven', moments in which you sensed that there is indeed a life after death, in which all must be fulfilled?

2. Have you ever accompanied someone on their last journey into death? What did you learn from the experience? Could you share that with others?

3. When you pray the Our Father, what particular thoughts come to mind with the phrase 'Thy kingdom come'? What aspects of God's kingdom do you long for most?

4. When you think over all the effort that goes into giving a dinner party, is there anything that helps you to understand how much God longs for us to be part of 'the banquet of heaven'?

5. Please read again the final quotation of this chapter. 'It is good for us to be here.' Please spend a few minutes, in quiet prayer, thanking God for the gift of the Mass. Could you share that prayer with others?

Prayer

Lord our God, you have given us the Eucharist as the memorial of the suffering and death of your Son, Jesus Christ. May our worship of the sacrament of his body and blood help us to experience the salvation that you give to us and the peace of the kingdom where he lives and reigns with you and the Holy Spirit, one God for ever and ever. Amen.

APPENDICES

APPENDIX I
A Year of Thanksgiving

*(based on the homily given in St Chad's
Cathedral at the Chrism Mass, 2005)*

In the final year of his life, Pope John Paul invited the entire Church to observe a special Year of the Eucharist, from October 2004 to October 2005. That year was marked in many different ways. All of them, however, corresponded to the invitation of the Pope that we should come to appreciate the Eucharist more fully and celebrate this presence of Christ with deeper interiority.

In a particular way, that Year of the Eucharist was a time of particular thanksgiving. 'Thanksgiving' is, of course, the first meaning of the word 'Eucharist'. This 'Eucharistic Year' is a good reminder that the first call and purpose of all prayer is to give praise and thanks to God. This is what we do today.

We give thanks first of all for the gifts of life and faith. They are fundamental to our self-understanding and to the way we go about our journey through life. We also thank God for the desire to know God, a desire planted in the heart of every person. It is this desire, sometimes not clearly recognised, that is the source of much of the restlessness we can feel. There is something within us which is always reaching out, always striving for more. Sometimes that striving is misdirected, especially when we are filled with a desire to possess an object, or even another person, for our own private benefit. But the restlessness that we feel can also give rise in us to a different longing: a longing to give ourselves, especially to that which we sense to be good, to be true, to be beautiful. This is our longing for God, coming to the surface in many different ways, in different expressions. We are restless; but our restlessness is answered in our search for God.

At a Chrism Mass, we give thanks in a particular way for the gift of the ordained priesthood, the gift through which the Mass itself is given to the Church. This is a wonderful gift to the Church, a charism through which some, chosen from the priestly people of God, minister to his people. It is the calling of the priest to serve the people of God in love, and to do so in a particular way: by offering the people the nourishment of the Word of God and the grace of the sacraments. As a Church we thank God for these sacramental gifts.

I never cease to rejoice in the affection and esteem in which we priests are held. Despite our failings we are given so much support and encouragement. This is so because, with the eyes of faith, we are recognised as men who have received the anointing of God and who have been given a role in the work of grace in the life of the Church and the world. Priests are grateful for this support and encouragement. It is the fruit of steadfast faith, for only faith can truly recognise and rejoice in the work of grace which comes about through the ministry of the priest.

Indeed, this faith, this recognition, points to the true nature of the thanksgiving we offer. We are thankful, quite simply, for the work of God in our lives – the *mirabilia Dei*.

Faith recognises the work of grace because the perspectives of faith have been shaped and nurtured by the Word of God. In the Scriptures, and in the Gospels in particular, these wonderful works of God are eloquently described. The bold Scriptural themes with which we are familiar portray for us the working of grace. It is to be seen whenever there is deliverance from slavery; whenever broken bodies are healed; whenever there is the forgiveness of sin and the gracious restoration of love and life. These are precisely what happens in the great Gospel narratives.

Yet, I suspect, the *mirabilia Dei* which we experience are not as clear-cut as the Gospel testimony. Ours are less dramatic than those portrayed in the Scriptures. The action of God in our lives is more hidden, immersed in our daily realities, woven into the fabric of everyday events and experiences. What is written loud and clear in the testimony of the Scriptures is often hidden in the small print of our daily lives. And so easily there it can remain, undetected and unappreciated.

For there is so much else taking place in our daily life that we are easily distracted from this subtle presence of God. Indeed, not only are there distractions, but also other texts are being written and presented to us, claiming our attention. These are texts which present other versions of salvation, of freedom, of fulfilment. Sometimes they catch our eyes and captivate our hearts.

Our world is particularly eloquent and persuasive in the messages that it gives us, about what is to be cherished, about what is important, true and helpful. Our world has its own gospel, its own message of 'salvation'. It is important for us to be aware of this.

In our culture today, in the air we breathe, there is a constant message telling us that God is absent from human affairs and, what is more, that God is not missed. We are told that, at long last, we human beings are autonomous. We have no more need of God. The truth propounded by our society, its secular gospel, unfolds accordingly. Salvation is our selffulfilment. 'Freedom' is a freedom from the constraints that others would seek to impose, and it is a freedom for me to exercise my choice at every moment. History is the story of progress, the inevitable unfolding, year on year, of better and better circumstances and prosperity. The notion of success contained in this message is the success which is prosperity, the prosperity which releases us from need and, most of all, from dependence.

In this secular 'gospel' truth is what we decide. In this 'gospel' we have the right to give meaning and justification to any course of action which we choose to follow. We rejoice in the autonomy of being able to do so. It is a measure of our independence, from one another, from outside control and certainly from any notion of God.

This freedom, autonomy, progress and personal truth are the things for which the world gives thanks. And, in all honesty, all of us have drunk deeply of this message. We have all raised a toast to success of this sort. We know we have. We see quite clearly that we have done so every time we complain about the circumstances, the demands, the consequences of our obligations which seem to constrain us in our pursuit of these aims.

But now we raise a different kind of cup. It is indeed a cup of thanksgiving. But in taking this cup we give thanks for quite different reasons and for quite different expectations.

For a start, the thanksgiving we offer here is directed entirely beyond ourselves and our own achievements. Our thanks, true thanks, is directed to the Father. In him we see and recognise the source, the sole source, of our well-being. We give thanks to our heavenly Father whom we come to know as our loving creator, as the fulfilment of all our longings, as the origin of all goodness, purpose, harmony and life.

Our thanks to the Father arise in and through Christ. He, we know, is the Gift of the Father and our Way to the Father. Our thanks, paradoxically, find their truest expression, their truest form, in that which gives shape to his life. Our thanks go to the Father in and through the one Sacrifice of Christ, his death on the Cross and his rising to new life.

Now indeed we understand the scandal of the Cross. Here, perhaps more than anywhere else, we see and measure how much we are at odds with the world around us. When we take this cup of salvation, when we raise this cup of thanksgiving, we reject the successes and thankfulness of the world's gospel. Instead we drink deeply of the Gospel of Christ, a Gospel proclaimed in its fullness on the Cross.

So today let us give thanks for what we are given, not what we have gained. We are thankful that we can follow the will of the Father, in obedience, rather than follow the pathway of self-determination. We are thankful – and how difficult this is – that our lives are marked by weakness and, at times, by suffering, for then we can be filled more readily with the goodness of the Lord. We are thankful even when we are 'persecuted', for then we are closer to our Blessed Lord in the deepest expressions of his love.

This is the small print we strive to read in our daily experience. It is so easily missed. How ready we are to interpret a successful moment as our own achievement rather than as God's gift. How quickly we come to view our duty and obedience as a burden rather than an opportunity. How quick we are to complain about our tasks and suffering rather than see them as the road to deeper union with the Lord. How ready we are to interpret unjustified criticism in the manner of an offended victim rather than see it as an opportunity to depend on God more completely.

This is the message of our Eucharist, our thanksgiving today. We are thankful to our heavenly Father for all the ways in which he draws us closer to himself along the path first trodden by his beloved Son. For that is the only pathway to life.

In a message to priests for Maundy Thursday, Pope John Paul II invited us to allow our lives to be shaped by the Eucharist we celebrate each day. This surely means that we must constantly give thanks. We are asked by the action of every Mass, to live a life of thanksgiving, alert to all the hidden and paradoxical ways in which the Lord graces our daily lives.

We are to see beyond the surface events, beyond the text which the world wants us to read. In the context of prayer, we are to search out the deeper meaning of our struggles and our anxieties. We are to discern the sacramental nature of each moment, the manner in which it is bringing us into the life of God. That is one reason why, in our daily lives, there must be oases of stillness and prayer. Only in such moments will we go beyond the surface of our experiences and find their inner truth, their sacramental heart.

In order to do this we are to be conscious of the particular temptation we face. For many this will be the temptation to dwell on indignation and anger, to be marked by cynicism and bitterness, for such are the negative hallmarks of the ways of our world.

Rather we are to be witnesses to the profound thankfulness which is the first and best stance of the disciple. In this we are not naïve, not indulging in some pretence that all is well in the world, or in our own lives. But, with the strength and perseverance of faith, we go beyond the troubled surface of our lives and bring forth its deeper treasure: that, hidden in every circumstance, there is an invitation from the Lord for us to grow closer to him each day. And for this we give heartfelt thanks.

Daily Mass is, of course, the fullest proclamation of this abiding presence of the Lord. We celebrate the truth of the Gospel: that Christ gives himself to us, to our history, in every time and place, out of his unconditional love.

So the Eucharist is never to be a brief half-hour at some point in the day. It should breathe life into every moment of the day, just as the presence of the Blessed Sacrament should breathe life into our churches. The Mass is never a tiny island of time on the edge of the day. Rather it is a summit and source of our awareness that in everything the Lord chooses to be with us, to stay with us and to be our joy and delight.

In this calling to be a people of thankful hearts and voices we are marvellously encouraged by so many others. How much inspiration we can draw from the courage and goodness of women and men who, in faith, accept the burdens of their circumstances, of their illness, of their old age with dignity, calm and even thankfulness in their hearts. Faith such as that can move each of us to seek to renew our own dedication, in the particular circumstances of our lives. Each day can be a new start. Each day, as we awake, we can set our hearts on the course of thanksgiving to the Lord and of unobtrusive service of others, especially those in need. Then we will be living the Eucharist. Then the Eucharistic Year will be fruitful in our lives.

APPENDIX II
Things to See and Understand

The Cover Image

The cover image endeavours to bring to a visual Cardinal Vincent's description of what it feels like being together in prayer when Mass is celebrated with one or two million people as described in the introduction to this book:

The crowds stretch beyond the horizon, yet the sense of being together in prayer during Mass is palpable. It is hard to describe!

One image may help me to do so. It is as if an underground stream has suddenly burst through to the surface and is there, before my eyes, in all its splendour and strength. That stream has been the unseen source of water and life for so many plants and flowers enabling them to grow and bloom on an apparently barren surface. This happens only because the plants and flowers have put down deep roots. When the stream suddenly becomes visible, then the source of all that wonderful growth becomes so clear!

Faith is that underground stream. So often it lies hidden under the dryness of our daily efforts. But occasionally it bursts forth. These great celebrations of Holy Mass are such moments, when the stream of faith in Jesus breaks forth from below the surface, cascading across a vast landscape of people, refreshing them and showing the true source of so much instinctive goodness that adorns our world. How marvellous are those grand declarations of faith in Jesus! How wonderfully he restores our energy and reveals the secret source of life! It is his divine presence which fills those millions of hearts, so that they begin their long journeys home with a totally renewed spirit and joy.

The Vestments

At Mass the priest wears vestments. Each vestment has a particular meaning. For example, the white alb stands for the purity a priest seeks in order to serve God with a pure heart. The stole worn around the neck and across the shoulders of the priest, both at Mass and whenever he celebrates a sacrament, represents the mantle of his ordination, the office of priest. He accepts the stole remembering the words of Our Lord: 'My yoke is easy and my burden is light' (Mt 11.28). The priest wears vestments at Mass in order to make it clear that here he acts not as an individual but as an ordained representative of Christ and the Church. At this moment, the personality of the priest is not that important. Here he is 'another Christ' rather than a private individual.

The Altar

As Mass begins you will see the priest approach and kiss the altar. This is an act of reverence, for the altar is the place on which the sacrifice of Christ's death is to be made sacramentally present. The altar is holy. It has been solemnly consecrated by the bishop, set aside for this holy task. The altar contains, either within it or below it, relics of a saint, as a reminder that, when we pray, the saints in heaven join in this praise of God. The top of the altar has five small crosses carved into the stone. These represent the five wounds of our Lord's body: his wounded hands and feet, and his wounded side. These wounds were made when Christ died on the cross. The altar is again going to bear the Body of Christ, being made present in the action of the Mass.

The Missal

The priest will read the prayers and the texts of the Mass from a large book or Missal. Sometimes this will be held for him. The Missal reminds us that it is the Church, the whole Catholic Church, which gives us the Mass. We do not make up the prayers as we go along. Rather, they are the prayers of the entire Catholic Church throughout the world. Indeed, the first prayer is called the 'Collect', for it brings together, for that day, the prayers of all the people of the Church throughout the world.

Processions

During Mass there are various processions. What do they mean?

The Entrance Procession represents the gathering of people for Mass. For practical reasons most people are in their places already. But the procession is a sign of us coming together. That's why it is led by a crucifix (at least on solemn occasions) because it is Christ himself who calls us together, who leads us as his people into the act of worship and sacrifice. Sometimes the Gospel Book will be carried in this procession because it is especially by his Word that we are called by Christ. The servers, deacon and priest are part of this procession for they will act on behalf of us all.

The Offertory Procession is where just a few people bring forward to the priest the bread and wine to be offered to God. They, too, represent us all, for the bread and wine are our gifts. They are gifts through which we offer to God all that we do, all that we have, all that gives us joy, and all our grief, too. Often the collection of money is part of this procession, for the cash is our gift, too. This gift is given as a sign of our love and support for the Church. Without this gift the Church, the parish, will not be able to keep going!

The Communion Procession is the one procession in which everyone can take part, going up to the altar for that particular sign of our sharing in the sacrifice of Christ which has just taken place. Everyone can go forward: some to receive Holy Communion; others, who are not able to receive Holy Communion for a variety of reasons, to receive the personal blessing of Christ given by the priest.

All the processions are expressions of the pilgrimage we make through life. But the Communion procession in particular reminds us that we make our journey together, helping and supporting one another, moving together towards Christ and strengthened by his gifts and his blessing.

The Final Procession. As Mass ends we are all sent out. The representatives go first, again led by the cross, out into the world. We all follow, conscious that not only has our duty to worship God been well fulfilled but also that we have received a mandate to be Christ's representatives, his messengers, in our world today.

In 597 St Augustine landed on the south coast of England. He had been sent by Pope St Gregory to preach the Gospel to the people of this land. As St Augustine came ashore he was led by a cross bearer, and the Book of the Gospels held aloft. That was how he started his mission. That is what we do, in the same fashion, at the end of every Mass.

During each of these processions there may well be singing. The hymns lift our hearts and spirits as we make our journey of faith through life.

The Responsorial Psalm

After the first reading we hear, and join in, a psalm. The psalms are the ancient hymns and poems of the Bible. They are some of the oldest prayers. We use them here as a response to the reading we have just heard. The psalms, which are either said or sung, can often express the feelings of our own hearts.

Standing, Sitting, Kneeling

At different times in the Mass we take up different postures. It's good to understand why.

Standing: This is a sign of our respect and attentiveness, and of our desire to praise God. So we stand at the beginning of the Mass to show respect for the priest as he enters, and to sing our praise of God in the 'Gloria'. We remain standing for the first formal prayer of the Mass, the Collect. We stand again for the Gospel in order to recognise the solemnity of the words being proclaimed and to salute a special presence of Christ in his Word. For the same reasons we stand for the 'Holy, holy...' which comes after the offertory, and for the time before Holy Communion, and again for the concluding rites and final blessing.

Sitting: We sit in order to listen attentively, and sometimes just to take the weight of our feet! During the readings and during the homily or sermon we sit in order to give our full attention to what is being said. It's not always easy to do so, but it's worth the effort!

Kneeling: Kneeling is the outward sign of the adoration we offer to God through the solemn Eucharistic Prayer of the Mass. We kneel in recognition of the powerful presence and action of the Holy Spirit, transforming bread and wine into the body and blood of Christ. We kneel in the presence of our Saviour. We kneel in recognition of our own unworthiness, in gratitude and in awe. We kneel, too, when we have received our Lord in Holy Communion, for he has come to us personally and we welcome him, embracing him in our hearts, speaking and listening to him in love.

If, for whatever reason, we cannot kneel, these can still be the dispositions of our hearts, conveyed outwardly by our stillness and reverence.

The Incense

Sometimes at Mass the priest will burn incense, in a container called a thurible. The thurible contains burning charcoal onto which the spices, called incense, are put. There are many things to understand here.

The incense is a traditional sign of the presence of God. The Christmas Carol, 'We three Kings' reminds us of this when we sing: 'Incense owns a deity nigh', which means that incense points to the presence of God.

The priest incenses the altar. The altar is a sign of the holiness of God and is the place where the sacrifice of the Mass will take place.

Later on the book of the Gospels will be incensed. This is to teach us that these are holy words, they are the Word of God, for in them God speaks to each one of us.

Then the gifts of bread and wine are incensed, just after they have been placed on the altar. These gifts are holy. They have been presented by 'the holy people of God' and they are to become the body and blood of Christ.

Then the priest is incensed. He represents Christ himself. He is a sign of God's presence.

Then the people are incensed. They, too, are holy in the sight of God. The people are the people of God, baptised into Christ, striving to live good lives and to bring the love and peace of Christ into the world.

At the moment of consecration, the priest holds up the sacred host and the chalice. They are incensed for the sacred host is the real presence of Christ and the chalice contains the blood of Christ.

Incense is a powerful sign, when we understand it.

The Bell

At certain points in the Mass a bell may well be rung.

The first ringing of the bell marks the start of the most solemn prayer of the Mass. In this prayer the Church requests that God gives, at that moment, the gift of the Holy Spirit to transform the bread and wine which we have placed on the altar into the body and blood of Christ. When that bell rings it is time to become additionally quiet, attentive and prayerful, for God will most certainly answer this prayer because Christ himself takes our prayer to his Father.

Just a little later the bells are rung again, after the consecration, as the priest raises up the consecrated host, the body of Christ, for everyone to adore. The bell is rung again when the priest raises the chalice now containing the blood of Christ for everyone to adore. Here Christ is truly present. We bow our heads in adoration of our Eternal King.

The words spoken by the priest at the moment of consecration include: 'This is my Body which will be given up for you', 'This is the chalice of my Blood,... which will be poured out for you...'. In faith we know that it is actually Christ who is saying these words. Christ speaks in and through the priest. The priest lends his voice to Christ so that Christ's words and actions may be made present in every part of the world, in every age.

The Hands of the Priest

If the priest has lent his voice to Christ, he has also given Christ his hands. So the hands of the priest are worth watching.

Sometimes they are held out in prayer. They express the love of the Son for the Father, and the love of the Son for us, his people. Just as Jesus stretched out his hands on the cross, so the priest stretches out his hands to express Jesus' embrace of his Father's will and Jesus' love for us all.

At one point, the priest holds his hands out, hands facing down, over the gifts of bread and wine. This is an ancient gesture which accompanies the prayer for the coming of the Holy Spirit. Just as the Spirit came down on the Apostles at Pentecost, so too we pray, with that gesture, that the same Holy Spirit will come down on these gifts.

At the end of Mass, the priest's hands will be raised in blessing. He will make the sign of the cross over all the people, thereby giving the people the blessing of God, the Father, Son and Holy Spirit. Jesus, we read, blessed the children that were brought to him. It is the privilege of the priest to make that same blessing present today.

Elevations

Four times during the Mass the priest raises the paten (the small dish or plate containing the host) and the chalice.

The first elevation is during the 'offertory prayers' by which the gifts of bread and wine are prepared for the sacramental sacrifice of the Mass. These prayers praise God for his gifts and offer to God the 'work of human hands'. The gifts are then solemnly placed on the altar. During these prayers, and this elevation, we offer ourselves to the Lord.

The second elevation takes place at the consecration. The priest solemnly raises the consecrated host – now the body of Christ – and then the chalice containing the blood of Christ. He does so in order that we may see and adore our Lord and Saviour. As he is raised before us we bow in prayer and in awe.

The third elevation takes place at the end of the central prayer of the Mass (the Eucharistic Prayer). The priest, often assisted by the deacon, raises the body and blood of Christ and says 'Though him, and with him, and in him, O God, almighty Father, in the unity of the Holy Spirit, all glory and honour is yours, for ever and ever.' We reply 'Amen'. This elevation is the climax of the Eucharistic Prayer, which sums up the loving obedience of Christ who brings us and all things to his Father. In saying 'Amen' we bind ourselves to Christ in his great prayer. We become one with him and, therefore, we are received and loved by our heavenly Father.

The fourth elevation is just before Holy Communion is distributed. Holding up the body and blood of Christ for us to see, the priest says: 'Behold the Lamb of God, behold him who takes away the sins of the world. Blessed are those called to the supper of the Lamb.' When we see this elevation we know we are invited to the banquet of heaven. This invitation is secure, beyond doubt, because Christ, the Lamb of God, has been victorious over sin and death. The next step of the Mass is to receive a promise of this future glory, in Holy Communion, or in a blessing, according to our situation.

The Breaking of the Sacred Host

Just before Holy Communion begins there is another important action to be seen and understood. But it is easily missed.

The priest holds the sacred host just above the chalice. He breaks it into two. He then breaks off a small piece of the host and drops it into the chalice, into the blood of Christ. As he does this he says: 'May this mingling of the Body and Blood of our Lord Jesus Christ bring eternal life to us who receive it.'

This solemn action reminds us again that the Mass is the celebration of the sacrifice of Christ. On the cross the body of Christ is broken. His flesh is torn, his side is pierced, his blood pours out. His death, and his rising from the dead, is the source of our salvation. His bodily sacrifice becomes the means by which all people, who share the same flesh and blood, are offered in love by Christ to the Father and received, healed, raised up by the Father in his turn. The breaking of the sacred host, the body of Christ, and the mingling of the sacramental body and blood of Christ show us how total his sacrifice really was, how totally he gives himself to us. In return we receive him with contrite yet loving hearts.

IMAGE CREDITS

Cover Image
© M_Bober/shutterstock.com

p129
© Mazur/Catholic Church England & Wales

p130 & 131
All photos © Sue Conway

p132
Top: © Sue Conway
Bottom: © Mazur/Catholic Church England & Wales

p133
Both photos © Sue Conway

p134
© Mazur/Catholic Church England & Wales

p135
Both photos © Mazur/Catholic Church England & Wales

p136
Top: © Sue Conway
Bottom: © Mazur/Catholic Church England & Wales

ABOUT THE AUTHOR

Cardinal Vincent Nichols, Archbishop of Westminster, was ordained to the priesthood on 21 December 1969. He served at St Anne's Parish in the Toxeth area of Liverpool and in 1980 was appointed Director of Upholland Northern Institute, an Adult Education College. He served for eight years as the General Secretary of the Bishop's Conference of England and Wales and was ordained Bishop of North London in 1992 and was then made Archbishop of Birmingham from 2000-09. In 2009 he was installed as the 11th Archbishop of Westminster and became Cardinal Priest on 22 February 2014 of Santissimo Redentore e Sant'Alfonso in via Merulana. He is the President of the Bishops' Conference of England and Wales and Vice President of the Council of the Bishops' Conference of Europe (CCEE).